The
Good-for-You
Garlic Cookbook

How to Order:
Single copies may be ordered from Prima Publishing, P.O. Box 1260BK, Rocklin, CA 95677; telephone (916) 632-4400. Quantity discounts are also available. On your letterhead, include information concerning the intended use of the books and the number of books you wish to purchase.

The
Good-for-You
Garlic Cookbook

Over 125 Deliciously Healthful Garlic Recipes

Linda Ferrari

Prima Publishing
P.O. Box 1260BK
Rocklin, CA 95677

Library of Congress Cataloging-in-Publication Data

Ferrari, Linda.
    The good-for-you garlic cookbook : over 125 deliciously
healthful garlic recipes / Linda Ferrari.
        p.   cm.
    Includes index.
    ISBN 1-55958-488-2
    1. Cookery (Garlic)   I. Title.
    TX819.G3F47   1994
    641.6'526—dc20   93-49713
                                                              CIP

    96 97 98 AA 10 9 8 7 6 5
Printed in the United States of America

To my good friend and computer wiz,
Sherry Davis.
I could not have done this book
without her expertise.

Contents

Acknowledgments

I want to thank Jan Townsend at the *Sacramento Bee* for doing an article that spurred Prima Publishing to contact me. A big thank you to Jennifer Basye at Prima for believing I could do this and to Karen Blanco and Andi Reese Brady for all the help and advice they gave me throughout this project. I want my agent, Linda Hayes, to know how much I value the help and knowledge she has shared with me. I also want to express my gratitude to Jane Gilligan at Bookman Productions for her help with the final steps of production and to the American Cancer Society for all the information they provided me.

I love the cover of my book and want to thank Lindy Dunlavey and Linda Fennimore for the beautiful job they did. And thanks to Paula Goldstein for the nice artwork on the inside.

There are many people involved on a project like this; it takes a lot of steps to get the final product out. Through it all, my family has been supportive. Thank you to my husband Phil, our children Philip, Michelle, Cindy, Suzy, Carrie, and T. J., and to my beautiful 83-year-old mother, Evelyn Walker, who is the inspiration behind much of my cooking.

I want to give special acknowledgment to the students who attend my cooking classes repeatedly and let me try new ideas and recipes out on them; they're really good sports.

Last of all, I want to thank Jill Presson for always being there to help me, and Georgia Bockoven for getting me into this business in the first place.

Introduction

People have been fascinated by garlic for thousands of years. Ancient documents mention garlic, and many folk stories and poems tell about its power. In years past, garlic was either worshipped or scorned. It was thought to have mystical powers against evil, especially against vampires. Even my grandmother, bless her heart, believed in its powers—she would eat crushed cloves on bread to ward off evil spirits. But all she really kept away with the smell were her grandchildren and friends!

Today, we are less concerned with garlic's mystical powers than we are with its medical benefits. The active ingredient in garlic, allicin, is thought to have a beneficial effect on many diseases. The Cancer Research Center is currently exploring the possibility that garlic may protect you from certain types of cancer. Garlic is also thought to improve blood cholesterol levels and high blood pressure. Other studies have demonstrated that garlic helps prevent blood clots, heart attacks, tumors, and common viruses like the cold or flu.

Personally, I'm pleased to learn that garlic has so many good effects because I've always cooked with an abundance of garlic. Garlic gives character to many otherwise bland dishes. When I teach cooking classes, people invariably wander in from the hall to see what's cooking, drawn by the alluring odor of sautéing garlic.

I've found in my classes and research that while people are interested in learning how to cut the fat in their diets, they don't really want to take the time to calculate the total grams of fat they use every day. A recent survey states that while most Americans are interested in hearing about health facts, very few actually practice what they learn. Current government recommendations suggest that no more than 30 percent of our daily intake of calories should come from fat. With these recipes, I hope to give you examples of how some simple techniques can lead to healthful, lowfat meals.

Cutting fat from recipes and keeping great flavor is sometimes difficult. After all, fat gives food flavor and richness. So many lowfat recipes are bland and flavorless that people give up trying to lower fat consumption, figuring they'd rather err on the side of flavor. But it doesn't have to be that way. The secret is learning how to alter ingredients by using lots of spices, trimming fat and skin from meat and poultry, and exchanging high fat ingredients for their lowfat counterparts. For instance, "lite" evaporated milk can take the place of cream for adding richness to sauces or soups. You can also use cooked and pureed vegetables, grains, or potatoes to thicken and improve the richness of a dish. Richness can also be accomplished by reducing liquids like broth, fruit juice, vegetable juice, or wine. Another easy way to replace fat is to substitute 2 egg whites for 1 whole egg or to use egg substitute. It's recommended that you limit your consumption of eggs to 3 times a week. Wonderful nonfat dairy products on the market today, such as fatfree sour cream, cream cheese, and cottage cheese, let us have the flavors and textures we are used to without the fat. I've had good luck baking with these products, but be very careful when using them on the stovetop. For instance, don't boil sauces made with these products, or they may separate and become watery. When you look for lowfat and nonfat ingredients on the market, make sure you read the labels. The meanings of *lite, lowfat,* and *skim* can vary for the same food product produced by different companies.

Since we are cooking with garlic throughout this book, here are a few tips to keep in mind:

- choose firm garlic with the paperlike covering intact
- store garlic in a garlic holder, which will keep your garlic fresh
- do not store garlic in the refrigerator (moisture is not good for garlic)
- remove the garlic smell from your hands by rubbing with salt or lemon juice
- remove the scent of garlic from your breath by eating parsley or sucking a slice of lemon

"Good-for-you" can be exciting, mouthwatering, and absolutely delicious as you'll discover in this book. These recipes should satisfy even the pickiest of eaters as they combine the tantalizing flavor of garlic with lowfat ingredients that don't skimp on flavor. Enjoy!

A note on nutritional data:
A per serving nutritional breakdown of each recipe is given in calories, protein, fat, carbohydrate, dietary fiber, sodium, and cholesterol. If a range is given for the number of servings or amount of an ingredient, the breakdown is based on an average of the figures given. Nutritional content may vary depending on the specific brands or types of ingredients used. "Optional" ingredients or those for which no specific amount is stated are not included in the breakdown.

The
Good-for-You
Garlic Cookbook

Vegetable Torta

Chicken and Beans in Endive

Artichoke and Chili Spread

Herbed Cream Cheese Spread

Lowfat Vegetable Dip

Sorrel Dip for Vegetables

Chinese Dumplings

Mexican Turkey Bites with
Creamy Salsa Sauce

Crab in Cucumber Cups

Shrimp in Lettuce Cups

Spicy Crab Cakes with
Roast Pepper Sauce

Spicy Antipasto

Stuffed Mushrooms with Rice

Artichoke and Dried Tomato Crostini

Tomato-Basil Crostini

1

Appetizers

Nothing is more comforting than having friends in to savor a relaxing drink and some delicious tidbits that kindle every one's tastebuds. I enjoy planning a well-rounded selection that leaves a lasting impression. Sometimes the results are so satisfying that to go on to anything other than these little delicacies would be unthinkable.

It's wonderful to be able to indulge in some garlicky appetizers that are also healthful and low in fat. Take a guiltless trip into pure bliss with the following recipes.

These appetizers can precede a full meal or graciously stand alone. Just have fun with it all and enjoy!

Vegetable Torta

This appetizer looks beautiful on a plate surrounded with a smidgen of Roast Pepper Sauce (see p. 17).

Makes 10 to 12 appetizer servings

	olive oil spray
2	cups carrots, sliced very thin
1	sprig fresh thyme
1	10-ounce package frozen spinach, thawed and drained
1	pound mushrooms, chopped
6	cloves garlic, minced
1	onion, minced
1	9-ounce package frozen artichoke hearts, thawed and chopped
3/4	cup egg substitute
1	cup nonfat cottage cheese
1/3	cup grated Parmesan cheese
1	tablespoon chopped fresh thyme
1	teaspoon *each* dried oregano and basil
1 to 2	teaspoons black pepper
	salt to taste

Preheat oven to 375°.

Spray a deep dish pie pan with olive oil spray. Put a sprig of fresh thyme in the center of the pan and line pan with a thin layer of the carrots. Put spinach in a bowl and set aside. Sauté mushrooms, garlic, and onion in olive oil spray until moisture from mushrooms evaporates. Mix with spinach. Add all other ingredients and blend well. Spoon mixture on top of carrots and smooth. Cover top with another layer of carrots. Spray top with olive oil spray. Bake until torta is semifirm, about 30 to 35 minutes. Let torta cool. This torta is equally good served warm, at room temperature, or cold. The torta is great alone but looks lovely with a little Roast Pepper Sauce.

Each serving provides:

79	Calories	11 g	Carbohydrates
8 g	Protein	179 mg	Sodium
1 g	Fat	4 mg	Cholesterol
3 g	Dietary Fiber		

Chicken and Beans in Endive

I really love hot and spicy food such as the following dish. Chili paste is sold in the Oriental section of most supermarkets and always in Oriental grocery stores. It is very hot so use it carefully. If Chinese basil is not available you can use regular basil, but Chinese basil has a slight anise flavor and lends a great taste.

Makes 32 servings

2	whole chicken breasts, boned, skinned, and minced
3	green onions, minced
6	large Chinese basil leaves, minced
	salt and pepper to taste
6	cloves garlic, minced
2	tablespoons minced fresh mint
2	teaspoons sesame oil
1	cup cooked white beans (see Basics)
1	tablespoon grated fresh ginger
1-1/2 to 2 teaspoons chili paste
1/4	cup rice vinegar
1/4	cup defatted chicken broth
3	tablespoons lite soy sauce
	fresh cilantro to taste
32	Belgian endive leaves (about 3 heads)

Combine chicken, onion, basil, salt and pepper, garlic, and mint. Sauté chicken mixture in sesame oil a little at a time until all chicken is cooked. Remove to a dish as it cooks. Return chicken mixture to pan when all is cooked and add beans, ginger, chili paste, vinegar, chicken broth, and soy sauce. Cook until liquid is almost absorbed. Stir in as much cilantro as you like. I love it really spicy so I add quite a bit. Spoon a tablespoon into an endive leaf and arrange on a beautiful plate.

Each serving provides:

32	Calories	2 g	Carbohydrates
4 g	Protein	76 mg	Sodium
1 g	Fat	9 mg	Cholesterol
0 g	Dietary Fiber		

Artichoke and Chili Spread

Makes 16 servings
(2-1/2 tablespoons per serving)

1	cup artichoke hearts in water, drained and chopped
1/4	cup diced green chilies
1/2	red bell pepper, chopped
1	tablespoon minced cilantro
1/3	cup tomatillos, husks removed and diced
6	cloves garlic, chopped
8	ounces fatfree soft cream cheese
2	tablespoons grated Parmesan cheese
1 to 2	tablespoons nonfat milk
	salt and pepper to taste
1	6-inch french bread round

Preheat oven to 375°.

Combine first 10 ingredients in a bowl and mix well. Cut a lid off the bread and scoop out the center of the bread. Fill the bread with the artichoke mixture and put the lid back on the bread. Wrap the bread completely in foil and bake for 30 minutes. When done remove foil and serve with sliced french bread, melba toast, baked pita triangles, fatfree crackers, or baked tortilla triangles.

Each serving provides:

24	Calories	2 g	Carbohydrates
3 g	Protein	103 mg	Sodium
0 g	Fat	3 mg	Cholesterol
0 g	Dietary Fiber		

Note: Analysis does not include bread.

Herbed Cream Cheese Spread

I use Vegit® in lots of my recipes to add low-calorie "punch." It can be found in grocery stores and health food stores.

Makes 10 servings
(2-1/2 tablespoons per serving)

8	ounces fatfree cream cheese
4	cloves garlic, parboiled and then chopped
1	tablespoon minced fresh chives
2	tablespoons minced red bell pepper
2	tablespoons minced parsley
2	teaspoons dried chervil
2	teaspoons dried tarragon
1	teaspoon vegetable seasoning (such as Vegit®)
1	teaspoon lemon pepper
1/8	teaspoon smoke flavoring

Blend well and serve with crackers, bread rounds, or bread sticks.

Each serving provides:

29	Calories	3 g	Carbohydrates
5 g	Protein	265 mg	Sodium
0 g	Fat	4 mg	Cholesterol
0 g	Dietary Fiber		

Lowfat Vegetable Dip

This is a great lowfat dip that is delicious served with vegetables, thinned and used as a dressing for potato salad, or on a baked potato as a replacement for sour cream.

Makes 8 servings
(2-1/2 tablespoons per serving)

1	cup nonfat cottage cheese
2	tablespoons fatfree cream cheese
2	tablespoons lowfat mayonnaise
2 to 3	cloves garlic, mashed
1	tablespoon minced fresh dill
2	teaspoons celery seed
1/2	teaspoon dry mustard
2	drops Tabasco sauce
1-1/2	teaspoons vegetable seasoning (such as Vegit®)
1	teaspoon rice vinegar

Blend all ingredients and chill.

Each serving provides:

42	Calories	3 g	Carbohydrates
4 g	Protein	184 mg	Sodium
1 g	Fat	4 mg	Cholesterol
0 g	Dietary Fiber		

Sorrel Dip for Vegetables

This is my spicy version of the common spinach dip that is so popular for vegetables and french bread. Sorrel is a favorite of mine and I love to use it in many sauces. It's available fresh from many grocery stores—if you don't see it ask if they will order it. If you have trouble getting it, use spinach with some lemon juice added. Sorrel leaves have a somewhat sour, lemony flavor.

*Makes 18 to 20 servings
(2-1/2 tablespoons per serving)*

1/2	cup sorrel leaves
1/2	cup parsley
1/2	cup cilantro
2	heads garlic, roasted (see Basics)
1	cup nonfat sour cream
1	cup nonfat cottage cheese
3	tablespoons reduced-calorie mayonnaise
2	tablespoons nonfat cream cheese
1/2	cup canned water chestnuts, minced
	lemon pepper to taste
	vegetable seasoning (such as Vegit®) to taste

Chop sorrel, parsley, and cilantro in a food processor. Squeeze garlic out into processor and pulse. Add sour cream, cottage cheese, mayonnaise, and cream cheese and process until all is well blended. Remove to a bowl. Stir in water chestnuts and season with lemon pepper and vegetable seasoning. You can serve this in a bread bowl and with vegetables, cooked shrimp, crab claws, and the bread cubes from the bread bowl. This recipe is also delicious with 1 cup crabmeat added.

Each serving provides:

41	Calories	5 g	Carbohydrates
3 g	Protein	93 mg	Sodium
1 g	Fat	2 mg	Cholesterol
0 g	Dietary Fiber		

Chinese Dumplings

I use a little tool (often called a "potsticker maker") to pleat the dumplings because I love gadgets, but it's not a necessity because it is easy to pleat the dumplings by hand.

Makes 30 dumplings
(1 dumpling per serving)

1	package round wonton wraps (often called gyoza wraps)
2	teaspoons sesame oil
2	whole chicken breasts, skinned, boned, and ground or minced
2	tablespoons minced onion
5	cloves garlic, minced
1/4	cup minced celery
1/4	teaspoon minced fresh ginger
1/2	cup rice noodles (soaked in warm water and chopped)
2	tablespoons lite soy sauce mixed with 1 tablespoon brown sugar
2	tablespoons rice vinegar
1/4 to 1/2 teaspoon chili oil
1/2	teaspoon white pepper
2	teaspoons brown sugar
	vegetable oil spray
1/2	cup defatted chicken broth
1	tablespoon lite soy sauce
2	cloves garlic, minced

Lightly cook chicken in sesame oil. Add onion, 5 cloves minced garlic, and celery. Sauté until celery softens a little. Put vegetables and chicken in a bowl and add ginger, noodles, soy sauce–brown sugar mixture, vinegar, chili oil, and pepper. Blend well.

Put a large teaspoon of filling in the center of each wonton wrapper and fold in half. Brush the edges of the wrapper with water. Pinch edges together and pleat. Continue with other dumplings, setting them on a sheet of waxed paper and being sure they do not touch each other, until all dumplings are assembled.

Bring 2 quarts of water and 2 teaspoons brown sugar to a boil. Add about 8 to 10 dumplings at a time and cook until dumplings rise to the top of the water. Stir now and again so they do not stick and never

continued on next page

let the water boil or your dumplings may open. After the dumplings rise to the top, watch carefully and cook 2 to 3 minutes more.

Let dumplings cool and then put into a nonstick sauté pan that has been sprayed with vegetable oil spray. Add the 1/2 cup chicken broth, 1 tablespoon soy sauce, and 2 cloves minced garlic. Cover and cook until liquid has evaporated and bottoms of dumplings are browned. Serve with light soy sauce or hot mustard.

Each serving provides:			
68	Calories	10 g	Carbohydrates
5 g	Protein	153 mg	Sodium
1 g	Fat	10 mg	Cholesterol
0 g	Dietary Fiber		

Mexican Turkey Bites with Creamy Salsa Sauce

Makes 35 turkey bites
(1 turkey bite with sauce per serving)

Salsa sauce:

1	cup diced fresh tomato
2	tablespoons diced onion
2	cloves garlic, minced
1	tablespoon minced cilantro
2	tablespoons diced green chilies
1	teaspoon sugar
1/4	cup fatfree sour cream
1	tablespoon reduced-calorie mayonnaise
	salt and pepper to taste

Turkey bites:

1-1/2	pounds ground turkey
1/2	cup minced onion
5	cloves garlic, minced
1/4	cup minced parsley
2	tablespoons minced cilantro
2	tablespoons bread crumbs
1/4	cup old fashioned oats
1/4	cup pumpkin seeds
1	4-ounce can diced green chilies
1	teaspoon salt
1	teaspoon cayenne pepper
2	egg whites
	vegetable oil spray

Mix all sauce ingredients and chill. Sauce can be pureed if desired. Makes about 1-3/4 cups sauce

Preheat oven to 400°.

continued on next page

Mix all turkey bite ingredients and roll into 1-inch meatballs. Put onto a rimmed cookie sheet that has been sprayed with vegetable oil spray and bake about 30 to 40 minutes or until nice and brown. Serve with fresh Creamy Salsa Sauce.

Each serving provides:

42	Calories	2 g	Carbohydrates
4 g	Protein	112 mg	Sodium
2 g	Fat	14 mg	Cholesterol
0 g	Dietary Fiber		

Crab in Cucumber Cups

Makes 25 cucumber cups
(1 cucumber cup per serving)

2	long seedless cucumbers
2	6-ounce cans of fancy crabmeat, drained
2	tablespoons minced green onion
2	tablespoons minced red bell pepper
2	tablespoons minced yellow bell pepper
1/2	stalk celery, minced
4	cloves garlic, minced
1	teaspoon lemon pepper
1/2	teaspoon salt
3	tablespoons tarragon vinegar
1	tablespoon reduced-calorie mayonnaise
2	tablespoons fatfree sour cream
	juice of 1/2 lemon
1/2	teaspoon dried tarragon
2	drops Tabasco sauce

Wash and score outside of cucumbers with a fork. Cut cucumbers into 1 inch slices. With a melon scooper remove center of cucumber slice, leaving bottom intact.

Drain crab and put into a bowl. Add all other ingredients and mix well. Mound crab into cucumber cups and serve.

Each serving provides:

17	Calories	1 g	Carbohydrates
2 g	Protein	118 mg	Sodium
0 g	Fat	10 mg	Cholesterol
0 g	Dietary Fiber		

Shrimp in Lettuce Cups

You can leave the shrimp whole and serve with toothpicks, or chop them, as I have done, and serve in lettuce leaves.

Makes 6 servings

1	pound shrimp, shelled and deveined, each shrimp cut in thirds
2	bay leaves
2	lemon slices
1	red bell pepper, charred and peeled
2	tablespoons lemon juice
1	tablespoon fresh tarragon
1	tablespoon fresh basil
3	cloves garlic, minced
1/2	teaspoon lemon pepper
1-1/2	teaspoons celery salt
1	cup nonfat yogurt
1/2	cup lite evaporated milk
2	tablespoons reduced-calorie mayonnaise
6	little center leaves of romaine or red leaf lettuce

Add shrimp, salt, lemon slices, and bay leaves to 1 quart boiling water. Cook until shrimp just turn pink. Drain and discard lemon and bay leaves. Immediately plunge shrimp in cold water to stop cooking. Drain shrimp.

Put red bell pepper in a blender or food processor and puree. Add next 9 ingredients and blend. Pour over shrimp and marinate in the refrigerator for at least 2 hours. When ready to serve, spoon into lettuce leaves and arrange on a platter.

Each serving provides:

127	Calories	8 g	Carbohydrates
16 g	Protein	400 mg	Sodium
3 g	Fat	98 mg	Cholesterol
0 g	Dietary Fiber		

Spicy Crab Cakes with Roast Pepper Sauce

These little cakes make a beautiful presentation served around a red pepper filled with the Roast Pepper Sauce.

Makes 15 small crab cakes
(1 crab cake with sauce per serving)

Roast pepper sauce:
1   whole red pepper, roasted (see Basics)
1/3   cup fatfree sour cream
2   tablespoons reduced-calorie mayonaise
2   teaspoons minced fresh cilantro
1   clove garlic, minced

Crab cakes:
1/2   pound cooked crabmeat
1   tablespoon pepper oil
1/3   cup thinly sliced green onion
2   cloves garlic, minced
1/2   teaspoon dried red pepper flakes
1/3   cup diced red bell pepper
1/4   cup diced celery
1/4   cup bread crumbs
2   egg whites
1   tablespoon minced fresh cilantro
       fresh ground black pepper to taste
1   teaspoon celery salt
       vegetable oil spray

Blend all sauce ingredients in blender or food processor. Makes about 3/4 cup sauce.

Put crabmeat in bowl. Sauté the green onion, garlic, red pepper flakes, red bell pepper, and celery in pepper oil 2 minutes. Add to crab. Stir in bread crumbs, egg whites, cilantro, black pepper, and celery salt. Make small rounds, flatten, and sauté using vegetable oil spray.

Each serving provides:			
47	Calories	3 g	Carbohydrates
4 g	Protein	124 mg	Sodium
2 g	Fat	16 mg	Cholesterol
0 g	Dietary Fiber		

Spicy Antipasto

Antipasto takes on a different flavor with this recipe. To cut out fat we are not using the oil and vinegar marinade that is customary to most antipasto. Instead the vegetables are marinated in a tangy brine that gives lots of wonderful flavor. Instead of the usual salami and cheese that accompanies antipasto, serve this with thinly sliced turkey and roast beef. It makes for a beautiful and delicious appetizer. You can also add some hot peppers, olives, and pickles to the plate if you like.

Makes 8 to 10 servings

1	cup broccoli (cut into small flowerets)
1	cup cauliflower (cut into small flowerets)
2	yellow crookneck squash, thinly sliced
2	zucchini, thinly sliced
2	carrots, cut diagonally
1/2	cup thinly sliced radishes
1/2	cup cherry tomatoes, cut in half
1/2	each red and yellow bell peppers, julienned
1/2	red onion, thinly sliced
1	cup water
1/2	cup sugar
1	cup rice vinegar
1	tablespoon mustard seed
1	tablespoon celery seed
1/4	teaspoon pickling spice
1	teaspoon turmeric
1 to 2	teaspoons salt
8	cloves garlic, minced
2	tablespoons minced parsley
1/2	pound turkey or smoked turkey meat, thinly sliced
1/2	pound lean roast beef, thinly sliced

Wash and prepare all the vegetables. Put water, sugar, vinegar, mustard seed, celery seed, pickling spice, turmeric, salt, and garlic into a saucepan and bring to a boil. Add vegetables and return to a boil. Remove from heat, cover, and refrigerate overnight, tossing vegetables in liquid to blend flavors. When ready to use, line a plate with fancy lettuce and using a slotted spoon transfer vegetables to platter. Sprinkle with a little fresh parsley. Roll up turkey and beef slices and arrange on top of vegetables in center of platter. Serve with french bread, melba toast, or fatfree crackers.

Each serving provides:			
185	Calories	22 g	Carbohydrates
17 g	Protein	422 mg	Sodium
4 g	Fat	40 mg	Cholesterol
2 g	Dietary Fiber		

Stuffed Mushrooms with Rice

*These mushrooms have a great, slightly nutty flavor from the brown rice.
Be sure to defat the chicken broth before cooking the rice. To remove the
stems from a mushroom, just hold the mushroom upside down in your
hand and press on the stem near the base, and it will pop right out.*

*Makes 12 to 14 mushrooms
(1 mushroom per serving)*

12 to 14	fresh large mushrooms
	juice of one lemon
1	10-ounce package frozen chopped spinach, cooked and drained
4	cloves garlic, minced
1	stalk celery, minced
1	carrot, minced
3/4	cup cooked brown rice, cooked in 2 cups chicken broth
1 to 1-1/2	teaspoons freshly ground pepper
1	teaspoon salt
1	teaspoon oregano
2	tablespoons minced fresh basil
2	egg whites

Preheat oven to 350°.

Clean mushrooms and pop out stems. Toss mushrooms with
some lemon juice and let drain in strainer. Mix all remaining ingredients except egg whites. Beat egg whites until stiff, then fold into
the rice mixture. Fill each mushroom, mounding the filling. Bake in
a 350° oven for 20 minutes or until lightly browned. Drain on paper
towels and serve warm or at room temperature.

Each serving provides:

33	Calories	6 g	Carbohydrates
2 g	Protein	352 mg	Sodium
0 g	Fat	0 mg	Cholesterol
1 g	Dietary Fiber		

Artichoke and Dried Tomato Crostini

This is a great way to use goat cheese. Even my children (who say they don't like goat cheese) love these.

Makes 25 crostini
(1 crostini per serving)

1	14-ounce can artichoke hearts packed in water
1/2	cup dried tomatoes, soaked in warm water and slivered
1/2	teaspoon smoke flavoring
4	ounces goat cheese
3	cloves garlic, minced
1	tablespoon vinegar
1/2	teaspoon salt
1	teaspoon pepper
1	teaspoon Italian seasoning
1	loaf french bread, sliced in 1/2 inch slices

Preheat oven to 425°.

Drain and chop artichoke hearts. Add all other ingredients except the sliced bread and blend well. I do not use a food processor because I want the topping chunky.

Put about 1 tablespoon mixture on each slice of bread and bake until they just start to turn light brown. This takes about 6 minutes.

Each serving provides:

63	Calories	9 g	Carbohydrates
3 g	Protein	158 mg	Sodium
2 g	Fat	4 mg	Cholesterol
1 g	Dietary Fiber		

Tomato-Basil Crostini

When I was in Italy we often ate these before a meal. I also love them at lunch to eat like a sandwich.

Makes 15 crostini
(1 crostini per serving)

3	tomatoes, peeled and diced
1/4	cup each diced green bell pepper and yellow bell pepper
1	cup cooked navy or white beans (see Basics)
1/4	cup slivered fresh basil
3	tablespoons minced red onion
2	tablespoons minced parsley
1	tablespoon balsamic vinegar
	salt and fresh ground pepper to taste
1	loaf french bread, sliced in 1/2-inch slices
2	heads of garlic, roasted (see Basics)

Mix tomatoes, peppers, beans, basil, red onion, parsley, vinegar, salt, and pepper together.

Grill or broil sliced bread on both sides until toasted. Spread bread slices with roasted garlic and top with tomato mixture.

Each serving provides:

86	Calories	17 g	Carbohydrates
3 g	Protein	163 mg	Sodium
1 g	Fat	0 mg	Cholesterol
1 g	Dietary Fiber		

Bok Choy Soup

My Favorite Mushroom Soup

Carrot and Zucchini Soup

Chicken-Vegetable Soup

Red and Yellow Pepper Soup

Cioppino

Gazpacho

Corn Chowder

Sorrel Soup

Minestrone

Potato-Garlic Soup

Potato, Leek, and Artichoke Soup

Wonton Soup

2

Soups

A pot of soup simmering on the stove invokes warm and loving feelings. Soups can also be gratifying and creative culinary feats.

I always tell my students that they should have no fear when it comes to creating soups. They are very easy to make, and as long as you have a good stock to start with, it is almost impossible to make a bad soup. Soup is nourishing, inexpensive to prepare, and so versatile that you can use many different ingredients. Soup is really fun to make and, as an added bonus, the aroma that fills your house is almost as pleasing as the first spoonful of the finished product.

Bok Choy Soup

You can puree this delicious and pretty soup before adding the noodles if you prefer a smoother soup.

Makes 8 servings

1	teaspoon butter
2-1/4	cups water
1/2	cup minced leek, white part only
4	cloves garlic, minced
4	baby bok choy, thinly sliced
8	cups defatted chicken broth
2	large potatoes, peeled and diced small
2	teaspoons dried chervil
2	teaspoons dried marjoram
1	carrot, peeled and grated
3	ounces dry vermicelli
	salt and pepper to taste

Put butter and 1/4 cup water in a soup pot and sauté leek and garlic slowly until leek and garlic just begin to brown. Watch carefully. Add bok choy, chicken broth, and remaining 2 cups water and bring to a boil. Add potatoes, chervil, marjoram, and carrot. Simmer 25 minutes. Add vermicelli and cook 10 minutes more. Season with salt and pepper to taste.

Each serving provides:

121	Calories	20 g	Carbohydrates
6 g	Protein	1,027 mg	Sodium
2 g	Fat	1 mg	Cholesterol
1 g	Dietary Fiber		

My Favorite Mushroom Soup

I long for cold weather so I can eat this soup. Actually you can make this lovely soup any time of year but certain things seem best at certain times, so I like to eat this in cold weather. This is a beautiful soup to serve at Thanksgiving or Christmas.

Makes 14 servings

1	tablespoon butter
3	leeks, white part only, thinly sliced
16	ounces mushrooms, thinly sliced
1/2	cup flour
1	cup nonfat milk
1/2	cup white wine
10	cups defatted chicken broth
4	white potatoes, peeled and diced
1	head garlic, roasted (see Basics)
1	cup lite evaporated milk
2	teaspoons dried fines herbes (available in spice section of the supermarket)
2	tablespoons sherry
	salt and pepper to taste
	fresh chives, chopped, for garnish

Melt butter in a nonstick pan and sauté leeks and mushrooms until soft. Stir in flour and cook until all white from the flour is gone. Stir in nonfat milk and cook, stirring, until smooth. Add wine and broth and continue stirring until smooth again. Add potatoes, cover, and simmer for 45 minutes.

When garlic is roasted, squeeze into a food processor or blender and mix with evaporated milk, fines herbes, and sherry. Blend well. Whisk into soup mixture. *Do not let soup boil after adding evaporated milk.* Simmer soup for 5 minutes over low heat. Season with salt and pepper to taste and garnish each bowl of soup with chopped chives.

Each serving provides:

125	Calories	19 g	Carbohydrates
6 g	Protein	761 mg	Sodium
3 g	Fat	5 mg	Cholesterol
1 g	Dietary Fiber		

Carrot and Zucchini Soup

Makes 12 servings

	butter-flavored vegetable oil spray
10	cups defatted chicken broth
2	cups julienned carrots
2	cups julienned zucchini
2	parsnips, julienned
2	leeks, white part only, thinly sliced
1	head garlic, roasted (see Basics)
1/2	teaspoon ground coriander
1	teaspoon crushed rosemary
1/4	cup chopped fresh parsley
1	cup uncooked white rice (optional)
	salt and pepper to taste
	vegetable seasoning (such as Vegit®) to taste

Sauté carrots, zucchini, parsnips, and leeks in butter-flavored vegetable oil spray and 3 tablespoons of the chicken broth. Cook until vegetables become limp. Squeeze roasted garlic into same pot and add remaining broth, coriander, rosemary, and parsley. Add rice now if you want it. Simmer soup for 45 minutes. Season with salt, pepper, and vegetable seasoning. Cook about 5 minutes more to blend flavors.

Each serving provides:

68	Calories	11 g	Carbohydrates
4 g	Protein	848 mg	Sodium
1 g	Fat	0 mg	Cholesterol
2 g	Dietary Fiber		

Chicken-Vegetable Soup

Baking the ingredients for this soup gives the stock a wonderful, rich flavor.

Makes 12 servings

Stock:

1	whole 3- to 4-pound chicken, cut up
3	whole carrots, cut in half
4	celery stalks with leaves
2	onions with outside skin, cut in half
2	large potatoes, peeled and quartered
2	large leeks, white part only, sliced
5	large tomatoes, peeled and diced large
8	large cloves garlic, minced
1/2	bunch fresh parsley
6	whole black peppercorns
3	cups vegetable juice

Soup:

2	carrots, diced
2	celery stalks, diced
3/4	cup diced zucchini
1/4	pound green beans, diced
1/2	cup peas
4	ounces uncooked noodles
1	teaspoon dried marjoram
1/2	teaspoon dried thyme
	salt and pepper to taste
	minced parsley for garnish

Preheat oven to 350°.

Put all stock ingredients into a roasting pan and bake for 1 hour. Next, put all baked ingredients into a stockpot and cover with water. Simmer 1-1/2 hours. Strain all stock and chill to degrease stock (see Basics).

Remove chicken meat from the chicken bones and dice. Pick out potatoes and carrots and puree. Stir into stock. Add diced chicken and all soup ingredients. Cook until vegetables and noodles are done. Sprinkle with parsley and serve.

Each serving provides:

205	Calories	28 g	Carbohydrates
18 g	Protein	308 mg	Sodium
3 g	Fat	53 mg	Cholesterol
3 g	Dietary Fiber		

Red and Yellow Pepper Soup

Makes 8 servings

2	red bell peppers, roasted and peeled (see Basics)
2	yellow bell peppers, roasted and peeled
5	tomatoes, peeled and diced
2	tablespoons minced onion
	vegetable oil spray
1/4	cup minced fresh basil
1	head garlic, roasted (see Basics) and garlic squeezed out
3	cups defatted chicken broth
	salt and pepper to taste
1/2	cup lite evaporated milk
	fatfree sour cream for garnish (optional)

Roast and peel peppers according to directions in the Basics section of this book. Chop peppers and tomatoes. Sauté onion in vegetable oil spray until it softens. Put peppers, onion, tomatoes, basil, roasted garlic, and broth into a soup pot. Simmer for 30 minutes. Puree ingredients in a blender or food processor. Return soup to pot and cook 10 more minutes. If you want a thicker soup, you can thicken with a mixture of water and arrowroot. Season with salt and pepper and stir in evaporated milk (you can substitute regular nonfat milk for lite evaporated milk). Cook on low heat for 5 more minutes.

Each serving provides:

68	Calories	11 g	Carbohydrates
4 g	Protein	415 mg	Sodium
1 g	Fat	3 mg	Cholesterol
2 g	Dietary Fiber		

Cioppino

Cioppino is a favorite winter soup in my family. This version is healthful and low in calories, while still being very hearty. In a beautiful soup tureen with the large crab legs sticking out, it looks appetizing and picture perfect.

Makes 10 servings

1   recipe Red and Yellow Pepper Soup (see p. 32)
1   8-ounce bottle clam juice
1-1/2 pounds fish (such as cod, halibut, or sea bass), cut into 1-inch
          pieces
1   pound shrimp, shelled and deveined
10   clams in their shells
1/2   pound scallops
4 to 5 crab legs (1-1/2 pounds)

Make Red and Yellow Pepper Soup, adding the 8 ounces clam juice to the recipe and omitting the evaporated milk. Add the fish and cook 4 minutes. Add shrimp, clams, scallops and crab legs. Cook, covered, until clam shells open, about 5 minutes. Discard any clams that do not open. This is good served with a loaf of french bread for dipping in the rich soup.

Each serving provides:

202	Calories	9 g	Carbohydrates
34 g	Protein	691 mg	Sodium
3 g	Fat	130 mg	Cholesterol
1 g	Dietary Fiber		

Gazpacho

Served chilled, this is an old favorite for hot summer months. It's divine made with juicy, homegrown tomatoes. If you can't find nice ripe tomatoes, you may want to add a little water to the soup. This soup can be left chunky, the way I like it, or you can partially puree it.

Makes 10 servings

4	large tomatoes, peeled and chopped
1	large cucumber, peeled, seeded, and diced
1	medium red onion, finely minced
1/2	green bell pepper, finely chopped
1/2	yellow bell pepper, finely chopped
1/2	cup diced radishes
2	celery stalks, minced
1	tablespoon thinly sliced green onion
1	tablespoon minced fresh parsley
1	teaspoon dried tarragon
2	tablespoons olive oil
2	tablespoons minced fresh basil
2	cups tomato juice
2	tablespoons balsamic vinegar
5	cloves garlic, minced
1	teaspoon Worcestershire sauce
2 to 3	drops hot sauce
	salt and freshly ground pepper to taste

Combine all ingredients well and chill. Can be served with a bit of nonfat yogurt or fatfree sour cream for garnish.

Each serving provides:

66	Calories	10 g	Carbohydrates
2 g	Protein	201 mg	Sodium
3 g	Fat	0 mg	Cholesterol
2 g	Dietary Fiber		

Corn Chowder

*If you are on a lowfat, low-sodium diet yet want a ham taste, substitute
2 teaspoons smoke flavoring for the optional ham bone.*

Makes 10 servings

1	teaspoon butter
2	tablespoons water
1	large onion, chopped
5	cloves garlic, minced
1	leek, white part only, thinly sliced
1/2	cup shredded carrot
1/4	cup minced celery
7	whole ears of corn, shucked
2	tomatoes, peeled, seeded, and chopped
4	large potatoes, peeled and diced small
6	cups defatted chicken broth
1	cup white wine
1-1/2	teaspoons dried thyme
2	tablespoons minced fresh cilantro
1	large ham bone or 2 teaspoons smoke flavoring (optional)
1-1/2	cups lite evaporated milk
	salt, pepper, and Tabasco sauce to taste

In a stockpot, sauté the onion, garlic, leek, carrot, and celery in the
butter and 2 tablespoons water. As the water evaporates, the onion
will brown. Watch this carefully. Add whole ears of corn, tomatoes,
potatoes, chicken broth, wine, thyme, fresh cilantro, and ham bone,
if desired. Simmer 1-1/2 hours. Remove corn cobs and ham bone. Cut
the corn kernels from the cob and return to stockpot. Remove what
ham you can from the bone and add to soup. At this point you can
puree the solids from the soup or leave it as is. Add the evaporated
milk and salt, pepper, and Tabasco to taste. Simmer 15 more minutes.
You can thicken soup with cornstarch and water mixture if you like.

	Each serving provides:		
186	Calories	34 g	Carbohydrates
9 g	Protein	659 mg	Sodium
3 g	Fat	7 mg	Cholesterol
4 g	Dietary Fiber		

Sorrel Soup

I buy sorrel when it is in season, chop it, and freeze it. If you cannot find sorrel, you may substitute by using 1/2 pound spinach and 2 tablespoons lemon juice but the real thing is best. Sorrel is a wonderful, sour-tasting herb and many grocery stores will order it for you if you request it.

Makes 12 servings

3	large leeks, white part only, sliced
2	tablespoons chopped chives
6	cloves garlic, minced
8	cups defatted chicken broth
1/2	pound sorrel, thinly sliced
1/2	head green cabbage, thinly sliced
1	cup chopped watercress
1/2	cup chopped parsley
1	bunch spinach, chopped
1	cup fresh peas
4	boiling potatoes, peeled and diced
1	teaspoon dried chervil
1	teaspoon dried marjoram
2	cups water
	salt and lots of freshly ground pepper to taste
1	cup lite evaporated milk

In a large stockpot, sauté leeks, chives, and garlic in 1/3 cup of the chicken broth. Watch carefully and add a little more broth, if needed, until leeks are soft. Add sorrel, cabbage, watercress, parsley, spinach, peas, potatoes, chervil, marjoram, remaining chicken broth, and water to pot and simmer for 40 minutes. Puree all ingredients and return to pot. Season with salt and pepper. Add evaporated milk. Cook 10 more minutes.

Each serving provides:

119	Calories	21 g	Carbohydrates
7 g	Protein	709 mg	Sodium
2 g	Fat	3 mg	Cholesterol
2 g	Dietary Fiber		

Minestrone

You can substitute any of the vegetables or beans in this recipe with your favorites. If you like a very thick minestrone, mash the beans before adding to the soup.

Makes 14 servings

1	tablespoon olive oil
1/2	cup minced onion
5	cloves garlic, minced
2	medium carrots, chopped
2	medium celery stalks, chopped
3	large potatoes, peeled and diced
5	tomatoes, peeled and chopped
10	cups defatted beef broth
2	large zucchini, diced
1	cup chopped fresh spinach
1/2	head cabbage, thinly sliced
1	10-ounce package frozen lima beans
1/2	teaspoon *each* dried basil and dried oregano
1	teaspoon dried marjoram
1	10-1/2-ounce can white beans, drained
1	10-1/2-ounce can kidney beans, drained
1/2	cup dry pasta shells
1/4	cup white wine
1/4	cup minced fresh parsley
	salt and pepper to taste
2-1/2	tablespoons grated Parmesan cheese

In a stockpot, sauté onion, garlic, carrots, and celery in olive oil. Cook until onions and garlic turn color. Add potatoes, tomatoes, and beef broth and simmer 1 hour. Add zucchini, spinach, cabbage, lima beans, dried herbs, white and kidney beans, pasta, wine, and parsley and cook until pasta and vegetables are done, about 12 to 15 minutes. Salt and pepper to taste and serve with Parmesan cheese.

Each serving provides:			
159	Calories	27 g	Carbohydrates
8 g	Protein	759 mg	Sodium
3 g	Fat	1 mg	Cholesterol
6 g	Dietary Fiber		

Potato-Garlic Soup

A rich and delicious soup. My cooking students all groaned when I first mentioned this soup because of the large quantity of garlic, but now it is a favorite recipe that I am asked for again and again.

Makes 10 servings

2	heads garlic, roasted (see Basics)
3	leeks, white part only, thinly sliced
	vegetable oil spray
8	cups defatted chicken broth
4	large boiling potatoes, peeled and chopped
1	cup nonfat milk
	salt and pepper to taste
2	teaspoons butter (optional)

Roast garlic according to directions in Basics. Sauté leeks in a soup pot sprayed with vegetable oil spray until leeks are soft. Add chicken broth and potatoes and cook about 20 minutes until potatoes are tender. Puree mixture in a blender or food processor. Return to pot and squeeze garlic cloves into soup. On low heat warm until garlic is completely blended in. Add milk. Salt and pepper to taste and cook 5 more minutes. Stir in optional butter if you would like a richer flavor.

Each serving provides:

124	Calories	23 g	Carbohydrates
6 g	Protein	845 mg	Sodium
2 g	Fat	0 mg	Cholesterol
1 g	Dietary Fiber		

Potato, Leek, and Artichoke Soup

*If you like a thicker soup, you can thicken this soup (or any pureed soup)
with a little arrowroot or cornstarch and water mixed. You also can leave
this soup chunky if you do not like pureed soups.*

Makes 6 servings

2	teaspoons butter
6	cups defatted chicken broth
1	10-ounce package frozen artichoke hearts, or 8 fresh, raw artichoke hearts, chopped
1	large yellow onion, chopped
2	leeks, white part only, thinly sliced
1/2	cup thinly sliced celery
6	cloves garlic, minced
3	large white potatoes, peeled and diced
1	cup plain mashed potatoes
	salt to taste
1/2	teaspoon white pepper
	vegetable seasoning (such as Vegit®) to taste
2	tablespoons brandy

Melt butter with 3 tablespoons of the chicken broth in a large
stockpot. Add artichokes, onion, leeks, celery, and garlic. Sauté
until onions and leeks are soft. Add potatoes and remaining broth
and cook until potatoes (and artichokes, if fresh) are done. Stir in
mashed potatoes. Add salt and pepper. Add vegetable seasoning to
taste. Warm slowly and add brandy, blending well. Cook slowly for
15 more minutes.

Each serving provides:

195	Calories	33 g	Carbohydrates
7 g	Protein	1,042 mg	Sodium
3 g	Fat	3 mg	Cholesterol
5 g	Dietary Fiber		

Wonton Soup

You can either tie the wonton bundles with chives, as I have done in the recipe, or you can just fold them in half and press them together. I like to make this soup at Christmas because the little bundles look like presents.

Makes 10 servings

10   cups defatted homemade beef broth (see Basics), using
       brisket below for broth
1-3/4-pound brisket, all fat removed
1   10-ounce package frozen spinach, cooked and drained
6   cloves garlic, minced
       salt and pepper to taste
1   12-ounce package wonton wraps
1   egg white mixed with 1 to 2 tablespoons water
1   bunch whole chives

Be sure to defat your beef broth. Finely chop the brisket used to make the beef broth, by hand or using a food processor. Put brisket, spinach, garlic, salt, and pepper into a bowl and mix well. Put about 2 teaspoons of the beef mixture on each wonton wrap. Brush wrap with egg white mixture. Fold closed and pinch ends together. Tie each wonton with a chive that has been dipped in boiling water. Continue until you have as many wontons as you want. Warm the broth and bring to a boil. Turn down to a simmer and add wontons. Let cook gently until wontons rise to the top of the broth and then cook 2 more minutes. Put 2 or 3 wontons in a bowl and ladle in some broth.

Each serving provides:

185	Calories	23 g	Carbohydrates
14 g	Protein	1,074 mg	Sodium
4 g	Fat	24 mg	Cholesterol
1 g	Dietary Fiber		

Oriental Salad Supreme

Mixed Vegetable Salad

Chicken and Snowpea Salad with
Creamy Lemon Dressing

Citrus Surprise Salad

Fruit Salad with Spicy Pecans

Pasta Salad with Grilled Vegetables

Garlicky Pasta and Crab Salad

Celeriac, Carrot, and Cucumber Salad

Potato Salad with Salsa Dressing

Red and Green Slaw

Spinach and Mushroom Salad with
Creamy Garlic Dressing

3

Salads

S alads have become a significant item on the American menu. Today, with our diet-conscious society, they are often seen as a main course instead of the insignificant side dish they used to be. The variety of fresh fruit and vegetables available today makes it possible to create phenomenal salads. Let's leave behind boring iceberg lettuce and molded salads. Instead, we can construct spectacular combinations with light and healthful dressings.

Most of the calories and fat in a salad usually come from the dressing. Here you'll find lowfat dressings that use fresh herbs, spices, and other lowfat ingredients to enhance the flavor.

All the salads in this chapter can be enjoyed with little or no guilt. The ingredients of a good salad must be fresh, cold, and diverse to be appealing. Spend some time in the produce section of your favorite grocery store and make up your own favorite combinations.

Oriental Salad Supreme

What a gorgeous presentation this colorful salad makes! It's also a great way to use leftover chicken.

Makes 8 servings

1	cup thinly sliced napa cabbage (cut into ribbons)
1	cup thinly sliced spinach
2	cups cooked and shredded chicken breast
1/2	cup shredded carrot
1/3	cup shredded daikon
1/2	red bell pepper, slivered
1	tablespoon slivered green onion
1/2	cup thinly slivered fresh pineapple
1	tablespoon sesame oil
2	tablespoons soy sauce
1/3	cup pineapple juice
1	tablespoon honey
4	cloves garlic, minced
1/3	cup nonfat yogurt
1	tablespoon reduced-calorie mayonnaise
1	teaspoon celery seed
	salt and pepper to taste
2	heads radicchio for garnish

Mix cabbage, spinach, chicken, carrot, daikon, bell pepper, green onion, and pineapple together in a bowl. Blend remaining ingredients together (except radicchio) and toss with salad. Spoon into radicchio leaves.

Each serving provides:

121	Calories	9 g	Carbohydrates
13 g	Protein	314 mg	Sodium
4 g	Fat	31 mg	Cholesterol
1 g	Dietary Fiber		

Mixed Vegetable Salad

A beautiful salad to serve on a buffet table. The vegetables must be very cold.

Makes 12 servings

1	green bell pepper, julienned
1	yellow bell pepper, julienned
1	red bell pepper, julienned
1/2	cup sliced mushrooms
2	green zucchini, sliced
2	yellow zucchini, sliced
2	tomatoes, cut into sixths
1	cucumber, seeded and julienned
1	bunch radishes, thinly sliced
2	carrots, thinly sliced on the diagonal
1	jicama, julienned
1	small red onion, thinly sliced
6	cloves garlic, minced
2	tablespoons sesame oil
1/3	cup rice vinegar
2	tablespoons soy sauce
1/3	cup orange juice
1 to 2	teaspoons dried red pepper
2	tablespoons minced fresh parsley
1	tablespoon minced fresh oregano
3	tablespoons sugar
	celery salt to taste
	freshly ground pepper to taste

Prepare all vegetables. Put first 12 ingredients into a bowl. Put remaining ingredients in a blender or food processor and blend well. Toss vegetables with dressing.

Each serving provides:

78	Calories	13 g	Carbohydrates
2 g	Protein	184 mg	Sodium
3 g	Fat	0 mg	Cholesterol
2 g	Dietary Fiber		

Chicken and Snowpea Salad with Creamy Lemon Dressing

This chicken salad is attractive and brightly colored. I often use food and cookie cutters to cut vegetables for salads into pretty shapes. These always bring smiles. For instance, I cut the bell pepper for this recipe into a little star.

I use a little Italian gadget to slice the roasted garlic in this recipe. It shreds and slices garlic and is made by ACEA.

Makes 6 servings

Salad:

6	half chicken breasts, boned, skinned, and flattened
1/2	cup nonfat yogurt
2	tablespoons nonfat milk
1	cup bread crumbs
1/2	teaspoon salt
1	teaspoon pepper
1	tablespoon chopped fresh tarragon
4	cloves garlic, minced
1	teaspoon Cajun spice
1/2	teaspoon celery salt
1/4	pound snow peas, blanched
6	cups salad greens (a mixture of lettuces and some spicy greens)
12	cherry tomatoes, cut in half
1	yellow bell pepper, slivered or cut into stars vegetable oil spray
3	cloves garlic, finely slivered and baked (see Basics)

Dressing:

1	tablespoon minced parsley
2	teaspoons minced fresh tarragon
1/2	teaspoon dry mustard
3	tablespoons lemon juice
2	tablespoons olive oil
2	tablespoons fatfree sour cream
1	teaspoon sugar salt and pepper to taste

continued on next page

Preheat oven to 375°.

Prepare chicken breasts. Mix yogurt and milk and put in a bowl. Combine bread crumbs, salt, pepper, tarragon, minced garlic, Cajun spice, and celery salt in a flat dish. Dip chicken in yogurt mixture and then in the bread crumbs. Lay the chicken on a cookie sheet sprayed with vegetable oil spray. Bake for 35 minutes, or until nicely browned and yet moist. Remove chicken and cool.

Leaving the chicken breasts intact, cut them into 1/2-inch slices. Between each slice lay a snow pea. Lay breasts on salad greens and garnish with cherry tomatoes, bell peppers, and baked garlic slices.

Blend all dressing ingredients in a blender. Drizzle salad with dressing or serve dressing on the side.

Each serving provides:

297	Calories	23 g	Carbohydrates
33 g	Protein	639 mg	Sodium
8 g	Fat	69 mg	Cholesterol
3 g	Dietary Fiber		

Citrus Surprise Salad

Winter is the perfect time for a stunning citrus salad. The garlic in the dressing adds a little spark I think you'll like. Remember that the optional avocado is high in fat. If star fruit, which is very pretty, isn't available, you could substitute with sliced pineapple.

Makes 8 servings

1/3	cup grapefruit juice
1	tablespoon pomegranate jam or seedless raspberry jam
1	tablespoon honey
1	tablespoon reduced-calorie mayonnaise
1	tablespoon fatfree sour cream
2	cloves garlic, minced
1	teaspoon celery salt
1	tablespoon poppy seeds
1	head Bibb lettuce
1	grapefruit, peeled and sliced into rounds
2	oranges, peeled and sliced into rounds
3	kiwi, peeled and sliced into rounds
2	star fruit, sliced into rounds (optional)
1/2	cup pomegranate seeds
1	avocado, peeled and sliced (optional)

Put first 8 ingredients in a bowl and blend with a fork. Chill at least 1 hour.

Line a platter with Bibb lettuce. Lay grapefruit, oranges, kiwi, and star fruit in a circle on lettuce. Sprinkle pomegranate seeds over all. If using avocado, place slices artistically around plate. Blend chilled dressing again and pour over fruit.

Each serving provides:

86	Calories	19 g	Carbohydrates
2 g	Protein	97 mg	Sodium
1 g	Fat	1 mg	Cholesterol
2 g	Dietary Fiber		

Fruit Salad with Spicy Pecans

The garlicky sugared nuts add an interesting twist to this easy fruit salad.

Makes 12 servings

2	17-ounce cans fruit cocktail, drained
2	15-ounce cans mandarin oranges, drained
1	fresh pineapple, peeled and diced small
2	red apples, diced with skin on
2	firm red pears, diced with skin on
4	cloves garlic, minced
	butter-flavored vegetable oil spray
1/4	cup sugar
3/4	cup chopped pecans
2	cups miniature marshmallows
2	cups fatfree sour cream
1	head curly-leaf lettuce

Mix canned and fresh fruit in a bowl. Sauté garlic in butter-flavored vegetable oil spray. Add sugar to pan and let sugar begin to caramelize. Add the pecans and mix well. Turn out on a piece of waxed paper. When cool, chop, and add to salad. Add marshmallows to salad and mix in sour cream. Mound salad in a big bowl filled with curly-leaf lettuce.

Each serving provides:

278	Calories	57 g	Carbohydrates
5 g	Protein	42 mg	Sodium
5 g	Fat	0 mg	Cholesterol
3 g	Dietary Fiber		

Pasta Salad with Grilled Vegetables

Makes 8 servings

1/2	each yellow, green, and red bell peppers
2	green zucchini, cut in 4 lengthwise pieces each
2	yellow zucchini, cut in 4 lengthwise pieces each
4	whole green onions, sprout end cut off
5	tablespoons bottled nonfat Italian salad dressing
8	ounces dry rotelle pasta, cooked and cooled in cold water, drained
7	cloves garlic, slivered and baked (see Basics)
1	tablespoon virgin olive oil
3	tablespoons rice vinegar
7	large leaves fresh basil, slivered
2	teaspoons vegetable seasoning (such as Vegit®)
	salt and freshly ground pepper to taste
1	head romaine lettuce, slivered

Preheat oven to 300°.

Put bell peppers, zucchini, and green onions into a bowl. Toss with Italian dressing. Grill vegetables, basting with dressing left in bowl, until vegetables are just browned and marked by the grill. Do not let the vegetables get too soft. Remove vegetables and dice. Put diced vegetables and cooked pasta into a bowl and toss.

Add baked garlic to pasta. Mix all with olive oil and rice vinegar. Add basil and season with vegetable seasoning, salt, and lots of freshly ground pepper. Serve immediately on some slivered romaine lettuce.

Each serving provides:

164	Calories	30 g	Carbohydrates
6 g	Protein	194 mg	Sodium
2 g	Fat	0 mg	Cholesterol
3 g	Dietary Fiber		

Garlicky Pasta and Crab Salad

A colorful salad that would be beautiful at a summer buffet or picnic.

Makes 8 servings

2   heads garlic, roasted (see Basics)
1/4   cup reduced-calorie mayonnaise
2   tablespoons fatfree sour cream
2 to 3   tablespoons vinegar
2   teaspoons sugar
1   tablespoon fresh tarragon
1   tablespoon fresh dill
1   tablespoon fresh parsley
1   teaspoon vegetable seasoning (such as Vegit®)
            salt and freshly ground pepper to taste
8   ounces dry pasta (such as penne), cooked and drained
1/2   cup diced yellow bell pepper
2   tablespoons diced green onion
1   large tomato, diced
1/2   cup cooked crabmeat
1   carrot, shredded
1/4   cup sliced black olives (optional)

Roast garlic and squeeze into a blender or food processor. Add mayonnaise, sour cream, vinegar, sugar, fresh herbs, vegetable seasoning, and salt and pepper to taste. Blend well.

Mix pasta with bell pepper, green onion, tomato, crab, carrot (and olives if desired). Toss with dressing and correct seasoning if necessary.

Each serving provides:

181	Calories	32 g	Carbohydrates
7 g	Protein	106 mg	Sodium
3 g	Fat	12 mg	Cholesterol
1 g	Dietary Fiber		

Celeriac, Carrot, and Cucumber Salad

Celeriac is an ugly vegetable but please don't let its appearance keep you from trying it—it's delicious. Celeriac will brown when peeled if not immediately put into an acidic liquid such as water with lemon juice.

Makes 6 servings

1	large whole celeriac (about 1-1/4 pounds)
	juice of 1 lemon mixed with 3 cups water
1/2	cup fatfree sour cream
2	tablespoons reduced-calorie mayonnaise
2	tablespoons rice vinegar
3	cloves garlic, minced
1	teaspoon celery salt
1	tablespoon minced fresh dill
1	teaspoon minced fresh thyme
1	teaspoon minced fresh tarragon
1/2	teaspoon pepper
2	carrots, peeled and julienned
1	large english cucumber, seeded and julienned
1	head Bibb lettuce
	fresh chives, chopped, for garnish

Peel celeriac with a sharp knife and cut into julienne strips. Put celeriac immediately into lemon-water mixture. Mix next 9 ingredients together to make dressing.

Toss celeriac, carrot, and cucumber together. Pour dressing over vegetables, toss well, and refrigerate at least 2 hours. When ready to serve, arrange lettuce leaves on a plate and pile the salad in the center of the lettuce. Sprinkle with fresh chives and serve.

Each serving provides:

90	Calories	16 g	Carbohydrates
4 g	Protein	244 mg	Sodium
2 g	Fat	2 mg	Cholesterol
2 g	Dietary Fiber		

Potato Salad with Salsa Dressing

Makes 10 servings

1   cup nonfat cottage cheese
1/2   cup nonfat yogurt
1/2 to 3/4 cup red tomato salsa (to suit your taste)
1   tablespoon chopped fresh tarragon
2   tablespoons chopped fresh cilantro
3   cloves garlic, minced
2   tablespoons tarragon vinegar
       salt and pepper to taste
3   pounds little red potatoes, cooked until tender and chilled
1   carrot, shredded
1/2   cup diced celery
1/3   cup diced red onion
1/3   cup diced green bell pepper
1/4   cup finely diced radish
       fresh cilantro for garnish

In a blender or food processor blend the cottage cheese, yogurt, salsa, tarragon, cilantro, garlic, and vinegar. Add salt and pepper to taste.

Cut up potatoes and add potatoes and remaining ingredients to a bowl. Pour dressing on and mix thoroughly. Chill before serving. Sprinkle a little fresh cilantro on top for garnish.

Each serving provides:			
148	Calories	30 g	Carbohydrates
6 g	Protein	199 mg	Sodium
0 g	Fat	2 mg	Cholesterol
3 g	Dietary Fiber		

Red and Green Slaw

*What a pretty dish for a Christmas buffet! If you do not want to take the
time to marinate the celeriac, you can substitute 1/2 cup diced celery.*

Makes 10 servings

2	cups shredded green cabbage
2	cups shredded red cabbage
1/2	cup julienned celeriac, marinated in 1/4 cup vinegar, 1/2 teaspoon salt, and 1/2 teaspoon pepper overnight before using
1/4	cup minced red onion
1	cucumber, seeded and julienned
1/2	cup fatfree sour cream
2	tablespoons reduced-calorie mayonnaise
1/2	teaspoon Dijon mustard
2	tablespoons rice vinegar
1	teaspoon caraway seed
2	teaspoons sugar
	salt and pepper to taste
6	cloves garlic, thinly sliced and baked (see Basics)

In a large bowl combine cabbage, drained celeriac, red onion,
and cucumber.

Whisk sour cream, mayonnaise, mustard, vinegar, caraway seed,
and sugar together. Season with salt and pepper to taste and mix
into slaw. Gently mix in baked garlic slices and combine well. Chill
at least 1 hour to blend flavors.

Each serving provides:

40	Calories	6 g	Carbohydrates
2 g	Protein	155 mg	Sodium
1 g	Fat	1 mg	Cholesterol
1 g	Dietary Fiber		

Spinach and Mushroom Salad with Creamy Garlic Dressing

Cut the sliced vegetables very thin (if you have a food processor use the #2 slicing disc).

Makes 4 servings

Salad:

4	cups spinach, washed and torn into pieces
1	cup thinly sliced white mushrooms
1/2	cup thinly sliced red radishes
1/2	cup thinly sliced celery
1/4	cup thinly sliced red onion

Dressing:

1/2	cup nonfat yogurt
2	tablespoons reduced-calorie mayonnaise
1	tablespoon frozen orange-juice concentrate
1/8	teaspoon smoke flavoring
4	cloves garlic, blanched and slivered
1	teaspoon celery seed
1	teaspoon lite soy sauce
1	teaspoon sugar
1/2	teaspoon dried tarragon
	salt and freshly ground pepper to taste

Divide spinach among 4 plates. Mix remaining vegetables together in a bowl.

Blend together all dressing ingredients. Spoon over spinach.

Each serving provides:

81	Calories	12 g	Carbohydrates
4 g	Protein	176 mg	Sodium
3 g	Fat	3 mg	Cholesterol
2 g	Dietary Fiber		

Green Beans and Red Peppers

Onions and Mushrooms

Zucchini with Garlicky Pesto

Stuffed Zucchini

Baked Artichokes

Baked Fennel

Crispy Baked Vegetables

Spicy Julienned Vegetables

Grilled Corn on the Cob

Creamed Spinach and Garlic

Pureed Carrots

Sesame Asparagus

Braised Hearts of Celery

4

Vegetables

W e can lower the fat content of our diet and become healthier eaters by making vegetables an important part of our diet. Garlic loves vegetables and lends optimum taste and benefits to an already healthful food. A visit to your local produce market or farmers market can give you many inspiring ideas—so much variety is available today.

Vegetables should not be cooked to mush. By combining marvelous colors and textures with quick cooking methods you can put vegetables into the spotlight on your dinner plate. Some of these recipes, such as the Stuffed Zucchini and the Baked Artichokes, make terrific one-dish meals that are genuinely satisfying.

Green Beans and Red Peppers

This dish will look beautiful on your Christmas buffet.

Makes 6 servings

1-1/2	pounds green beans, blanched
1/4	cup minced onion
4	cloves garlic, minced
1/2	cup defatted chicken broth
1	large red bell pepper, roasted (see Basics)
1	teaspoon butter
	butter-flavored vegetable oil spray
1	red bell pepper, julienned
	salt and pepper to taste

Blanch green beans and set aside. Slowly cook onion and garlic in chicken broth until broth evaporates. Puree onion mixture, roasted bell pepper, and butter. In a nonstick pan sprayed with butter-flavored vegetable oil spray, sauté julienned bell pepper for 2 minutes. Add green beans and pureed mixture and cook until beans are hot. Season with salt and pepper to taste.

Each serving provides:

58	Calories	11 g	Carbohydrates
3 g	Protein	97 mg	Sodium
1 g	Fat	2 mg	Cholesterol
3 g	Dietary Fiber		

Onions and Mushrooms

A wonderfully spicy side dish that's best served with a plain meat, fish, or chicken dish. It's even a great accompaniment to a plain turkey burger.

Makes 6 servings

1	pound pearl onions
1	pound small mushrooms, left whole
1	tomato, peeled and diced
6	cloves garlic, skinned and left whole
1	cup red wine
3/4	cup defatted beef broth
2	tablespoons tomato paste
2	teaspoons dried thyme
2	teaspoons dried parsley
1/4	cup lite evaporated milk
	salt and pepper to taste
	fresh parsley, minced, for garnish

Put onions in boiling water for 3 minutes. Drain, peel, and cut tops and bottoms off. Put onions in a small saucepan and add mushrooms, tomato, and garlic. Add next 5 ingredients. Cover pan and simmer for 20 minutes. Remove cover and let cook 10 more minutes. Stir in evaporated milk and salt and pepper to taste. Simmer for 5 more minutes. Sprinkle with fresh parsley.

Each serving provides:

75	Calories	15 g	Carbohydrates
4 g	Protein	172 mg	Sodium
1 g	Fat	2 mg	Cholesterol
1 g	Dietary Fiber		

Zucchini with Garlicky Pesto

Makes 8 servings

4 cups julienned zucchini
1/4 cup fresh basil
1/4 cup fresh parsley
1/4 cup canned water chestnuts
6 cloves garlic
1/4 cup fatfree sour cream
2 tablespoons nonfat milk
  salt and pepper to taste
1 tablespoon grated Parmesan cheese

Cook zucchini in lightly salted boiling water until al dente. Put basil, parsley, water chestnuts, and garlic in a food processor or blender and puree. Put puree into a pan, add sour cream and milk, and warm. Season with salt and pepper. Toss hot zucchini with warm pesto and sprinkle with Parmesan cheese.

Each serving provides:

26	Calories	4 g	Carbohydrates
2 g	Protein	22 mg	Sodium
0 g	Fat	1 mg	Cholesterol
0 g	Dietary Fiber		

Stuffed Zucchini

You can make a meal out of this zucchini recipe. Meat lovers can also add 1/2 cup cooked minced sirloin, turkey, ham, or chicken to the stuffing.

Makes 8 side-dish and 4 main-dish servings

4	medium zucchini
1	cup finely diced sourdough bread
1/2	teaspoon *each* salt and pepper
1/2	teaspoon *each* dried sage, oregano, basil, and parsley
2	tablespoons defatted chicken broth
1	tablespoon minced onion
1	tablespoon minced celery
1	tablespoon minced green bell pepper
4	cloves garlic, minced
1/4	cup egg substitute
1	tablespoon flour
1/2	cup lite evaporated milk
	vegetable oil spray
2	tablespoons freshly grated Parmesan cheese

Preheat oven to 350°.

Cut ends off zucchini. Cut each zucchini in half lengthwise and scoop out center of each. Parboil zucchini for 5 minutes. Rinse under cold water and drain on paper towels.

In a bowl mix bread cubes, salt, pepper, and herbs. Put the 2 tablespoons chicken broth in a nonstick pan and cook onion, celery, bell pepper, and garlic until liquid has evaporated. Add vegetables to bread cubes. Stir in egg substitute. Set aside.

Put flour and milk in a little container and shake to combine. Pour milk mixture into a little pan and slowly cook until it thickens. Stir into bread mixture. Stuff each zucchini half with mixture and lay zucchini halves side by side in a baking dish that has been sprayed with vegetable oil spray. Sprinkle with Parmesan cheese and bake for 20 to 30 minutes or until lightly browned.

Each side-dish serving provides:

61	Calories	9 g	Carbohydrates
4 g	Protein	249 mg	Sodium
1 g	Fat	4 mg	Cholesterol
1 g	Dietary Fiber		

Baked Artichokes

These delicious artichokes are a favorite with my family. I make a big plate of them spiced up with lots of pepper. We eat them with french bread topped with roasted garlic (see Basics). It's heaven!

Makes 8 servings

4	large artichokes
	vegetable oil spray
1	head garlic, separated into cloves and peeled
	vegetable seasoning (such as Vegit®)
	freshly ground pepper, to taste
1	tablespoon minced fresh oregano
16	whole mint leaves
4	cups defatted beef broth
1/2	cup white wine

Preheat oven to 425°.

Cut tops off artichokes and remove outer 2 layers of leaves. Snip tops off other leaves and then cut artichokes in half. Spray a baking pan with vegetable oil spray and lay artichokes, cut side down, in pan. Lay garlic cloves around artichokes. Sprinkle artichokes with vegetable seasoning, pepper, and half the oregano. Spread mint leaves over artichokes. Pour broth and wine over all and cover pan tightly. Bake for 30 minutes. Turn artichokes over and sprinkle this side with vegetable seasoning, pepper, and the rest of the oregano. Bake 20 more minutes uncovered. Turn artichokes again and bake about 5 more minutes until all liquid has evaporated.

Each serving provides:

58	Calories	11 g	Carbohydrates
4 g	Protein	475 mg	Sodium
1 g	Fat	0 mg	Cholesterol
3 g	Dietary Fiber		

Baked Fennel

Fennel is one of my favorite vegetables baked or raw.

Makes 6 servings

3   large fennel bulbs (about 2-1/2 pounds)
      vegetable oil spray
3   large cloves garlic, chopped
1/2   teaspoon crushed dried oregano
1/2   teaspoon crushed dried basil
1/2   teaspoon vegetable seasoning (such as Vegit®)
1/2   teaspoon white pepper
1 to 1-1/2 cups defatted chicken broth
2   tablespoons bread crumbs
      butter-flavored vegetable oil spray

Preheat oven to 375°.

Cut tops off fennel bulbs and cut each bulb in half. Spray an 8-inch square baking pan with vegetable oil spray. Lay the fennel bulbs, cut side down, in the pan. Sprinkle the fennel with garlic, oregano, basil, vegetable seasoning, and white pepper. Pour 1 cup chicken broth in the pan and cover tightly with foil. Bake for 15 minutes. Turn fennel over and bake covered, 15 minutes more. Add more chicken broth if necessary to keep the bottom of the pan from burning the fennel. Uncover fennel and sprinkle with bread crumbs. Spray crumbs with butter-flavored vegetable oil spray and turn oven up to 450°. Bake until bread crumbs are browned.

Each serving provides:

46	Calories	7 g	Carbohydrates
3 g	Protein	378 mg	Sodium
1 g	Fat	0 mg	Cholesterol
1 g	Dietary Fiber		

Crispy Baked Vegetables

These vegetables are great dipped in the Lowfat Vegetable Dip (p. 9). Baking parchment can be found in specialty food stores.

Makes 4 servings

1/2	cup seasoned bread crumbs
1/2	cup cornmeal
2	tablespoons grated Parmesan cheese
8	cloves garlic, minced
	vegetable oil spray
1	cup nonfat yogurt
1	pound of vegetables (zucchini, okra, eggplant, potato, sweet potato, mushrooms, parsnips, and/or onions)

Preheat oven to 425°.

Mix the bread crumbs, cornmeal, and cheese together.

Over very low heat, slowly sauté garlic in a nonstick pan sprayed with some vegetable oil spray until garlic begins to brown. Let cool and mix into crumb mixture.

Slice vegetables about 1/2-inch thick and dip them into the yogurt and then into the crumb mixture. Lay vegetables on a parchment-lined cookie sheet and bake until browned and crispy. Potatoes will take longer than other vegetables so be sure to cut them thin.

Each serving provides:

217	Calories	40 g	Carbohydrates
10 g	Protein	495 mg	Sodium
2 g	Fat	3 mg	Cholesterol
3 g	Dietary Fiber		

Spicy Julienned Vegetables

Black sesame seeds can be found in specialty food shops or Oriental grocery stores.

Makes 8 servings

2	teaspoons sesame oil
4	cloves garlic, minced
1	teaspoon red pepper flakes
1/4	cup defatted chicken broth
1	cup julienned carrot
1	cup julienned broccoli stalks
2	small bok choy, julienned
1	cup julienned parsnips
1	cup julienned red bell pepper
1	teaspoon butter sprinkles
	vegetable seasoning (such as Vegit®) and pepper to taste
1	teaspoon black sesame seeds

Sauté garlic and red pepper flakes in sesame oil for 3 minutes. Add chicken broth and vegetables. Cover pan and cook until vegetables are tender. Toss with butter sprinkles. Season with vegetable seasoning and pepper and sprinkle with black sesame seeds.

Each serving provides:

44	Calories	7 g	Carbohydrates
1 g	Protein	76 mg	Sodium
2 g	Fat	0 mg	Cholesterol
2 g	Dietary Fiber		

Grilled Corn on the Cob

I love outdoor barbecues because all the cooking can be done outdoors and there are so few dishes to wash. Grilling corn also gives it a delightful smoky flavor.

Makes 8 servings

8	ears of corn
4	teaspoons butter
2	teaspoons dried marjoram
1-1/2	teaspoons cayenne
4	cloves garlic, chopped
1	teaspoon salt
	dash of paprika

Remove silk from corn, keeping husks intact. Soak corn in water for 20 minutes. Rub each ear of corn with 1/2 teaspoon butter and sprinkle with marjoram, cayenne, garlic, salt, and paprika. Pull husks up to cover corn and grill 10 to 15 minutes, depending on hotness of coals, turning often.

Each serving provides:

98	Calories	18 g	Carbohydrates
3 g	Protein	309 mg	Sodium
3 g	Fat	5 mg	Cholesterol
3 g	Dietary Fiber		

Creamed Spinach and Garlic

Makes 8 servings

1	head garlic, roasted (see Basics)
	vegetable oil spray
1	cup minced celery
1	tablespoon minced walnuts
3	cups cooked spinach (drained and chopped)
1/3	cup fatfree sour cream
1	tablespoon reduced-calorie mayonnaise
1	teaspoon ground nutmeg
	vegetable seasoning (such as Vegit®) and pepper to taste

Roast garlic and set aside. In a nonstick pan sprayed with vegetable oil spray, sauté celery and walnuts for 4 minutes. Stir in spinach, blend and warm. Stir in sour cream and mayonnaise and mix well. Carefully warm mixture over low heat and season with nutmeg, vegetable seasoning, and pepper.

Each serving provides:

53	Calories	7 g	Carbohydrates
4 g	Protein	98 mg	Sodium
2 g	Fat	1 mg	Cholesterol
2 g	Dietary Fiber		

Pureed Carrots

For a special dinner party these carrots are very pretty squeezed through a pastry bag into small cooked zucchini boats.

Makes 4 servings

6	carrots, peeled
6	cloves garlic, minced
1/4	cup brown sugar
1	tablespoon fatfree cream cheese
1	tablespoon fatfree sour cream
1	tablespoon Madeira
1	teaspoon dried thyme
	salt and pepper to taste

Combine carrots, garlic, and brown sugar in a saucepan and just cover with water. Cook until carrots are tender. Drain and puree in a blender or food processor. Stir in remaining ingredients and blend well.

Each serving provides:

118	Calories	27 g	Carbohydrates
2 g	Protein	72 mg	Sodium
0 g	Fat	1 mg	Cholesterol
3 g	Dietary Fiber		

Sesame Asparagus

Use the best quality butter you can find in this recipe.

Makes 6 servings

2	pounds asparagus
5	cloves garlic, chopped
2	teaspoons butter
1	tablespoon sesame seeds
	vegetable seasoning (such as Vegit®) to taste
	freshly ground pepper to taste

Clean asparagus, break off the woody bottom portions of the stalks, and discard. Dice tops into large pieces. Set aside.

Sauté garlic in butter, in a nonstick pan, very slowly until garlic just begins to turn brown. Add a couple tablespoons of water and asparagus to pan. Cover and cook for 2 minutes, stirring frequently. If you like your asparagus softer, continue cooking until asparagus is done to your satisfaction. Add a little more water if necessary. When asparagus is done water should almost be cooked away. Sprinkle with sesame seeds and vegetable seasoning and pepper to taste.

Each serving provides:

41	Calories	4 g	Carbohydrates
3 g	Protein	15 mg	Sodium
2 g	Fat	3 mg	Cholesterol
1 g	Dietary Fiber		

Braised Hearts of Celery

Braised vegetables have a special, rich flavor. You could try this recipe using other root vegetables such as fennel, parsnips, carrots, and onions.

Makes 6 servings

3   celery hearts, cut in half lengthwise
4   cloves garlic, minced
      vegetable oil spray
      vegetable seasoning (such as Vegit®) to taste
      pepper to taste
1 to 1-1/2 cups defatted beef broth
1/2   cup white wine
3   teaspoons grated Parmesan cheese
      chopped fresh parsley for garnish

Sauté celery hearts and garlic in a nonstick pan sprayed with vegetable oil spray until celery is a little brown. Sprinkle celery with vegetable seasoning and pepper to taste. Pour 1 cup of the beef broth and the wine over the celery. Cover the pan and cook slowly until celery is tender, about 20 to 30 minutes. Add more broth if needed. Uncover pan and continue to cook until liquid has evaporated. Sprinkle with Parmesan cheese and put under the broiler until cheese has lightly browned. Sprinkle with fresh parsley and serve.

Each serving provides:

29	Calories	4 g	Carbohydrates
2 g	Protein	263 mg	Sodium
1 g	Fat	1 mg	Cholesterol
1 g	Dietary Fiber		

Crispy Baked Fish

Fish in Parchment

Pastry-Wrapped Fish with Mustard Sauce

Italian Fish

Grilled Trout with Cucumber Sauce

Grilled Orange Roughy in Orange Sauce

Grilled Fish with Mango Salsa

*Poached Salmon Steaks with
Creamy Cucumber-Dill Sauce*

Crab Puff Bake

Shrimp and Garlic

Hawaiian Shrimp

Shellfish Stirfry

*Shrimp and Halibut Bake with
Creamy Wine Sauce*

*Sole and Scallop Mousse with
Yellow Pepper Sauce*

5

Fish and Shellfish

F ish is a great lowfat, high-protein food. Some nutrition experts suggest that we eat at least 3 fish meals a week. (Shrimp, which is high in cholesterol, is the one exception; if you are trying to limit your cholesterol intake, eat shrimp no more than once a week.) But many people think of fish as bland tasting and difficult to prepare. Are they ever wrong! Most fish and shellfish blend beautifully with garlic and herbs, so use them in abundance.

It can also be incredibly fast to prepare. Fish is excellent just marinated in lemon juice, garlic and spices and then grilled or broiled. Remember never to overcook fish, because it will become dry.

It's easy to make wonderful sauces for fish with the nonfat dairy products available. Fish is also delicious with lowfat tomato-based sauces, such as the Italian Fish recipe in this chapter.

Fish can be made dramatic in pastries, sensational in sauces, and outstanding in stirfrys. Give it a chance and I think even those of you who have avoided fish in the past will realize how delicious and easy to prepare it can be.

Crispy Baked Fish

You can also use this crisp and tasty coating on chicken, turkey pieces, or pork chops.

Makes 4 servings

4	4-ounce pieces fish (such as flounder, sole, orange roughy, snapper, trout, or catfish)
	juice of 2 lemons
1/4	cup egg substitute
3	tablespoons water
4	cloves garlic, minced
1/2	cup flour
1/2	cup bread crumbs
1/2	teaspoon *each* dried oregano, basil, paprika, and thyme
1	teaspoon lemon rind
1/2	teaspoon salt
2	teaspoons Cajun spice
	butter-flavored vegetable oil spray

Preheat oven to 425°.

Put fish in a dish and rub with lemon juice. Let marinate while you prepare the rest of the ingredients. Mix egg substitute, water, and garlic together. Set aside. In another bowl put flour. In a third bowl mix bread crumbs, herbs, lemon rind, salt, and Cajun spice.

Dip fish into egg substitute mixture and then into flour. Dip into egg substitute mixture again and then into bread crumb mixture. Lay fish on a cookie sheet that has been sprayed with butter-flavored vegetable oil spray. Spray the top of the fish with butter-flavored vegetable oil spray.

Bake fish for about 6 minutes, turn fish over, and spray again with butter-flavored vegetable oil spray. Bake another 6 minutes, or until fish flakes and is done.

Each serving provides:

240	Calories	26 g	Carbohydrates
26 g	Protein	925 mg	Sodium
3 g	Fat	54 mg	Cholesterol
1 g	Dietary Fiber		

Fish in Parchment

Baking fish in parchment is a great way to cook without fat and makes a very dramatic presentation at the table. Baking parchment can be found in specialty food stores. Even though the alcohol in the brandy cooks out, its flavor is an important part of this dish. I recommend using a good quality brandy for best results.

Makes 4 servings

4	small red snapper fillets (1 pound total)
1/2	cup cooked crabmeat
1/2	cup sliced mushrooms
1/4	cup chopped green onions
3	cloves garlic, minced
	butter-flavored vegetable oil spray
1/2	teaspoon fresh tarragon
1/2	teaspoon Dijon mustard
4	tablespoons fatfree cream cheese
1	tablespoon reduced-calorie mayonnaise
2	teaspoons butter sprinkles
2	teaspoons lemon juice
2	tablespoons brandy
1/3	cup chopped parsley
	salt and freshly ground pepper to taste

Preheat oven to 375°.

Take 4 10-inch parchment squares, fold them in half, and cut them into hearts. Lay each fillet on a parchment heart.

Put crabmeat in a bowl. Sauté mushrooms, green onions, and garlic in a nonstick pan sprayed with butter-flavored vegetable oil spray, until vegetables are soft. Add to crab.

In a blender or food processor mix tarragon, mustard, cream cheese, mayonnaise, butter sprinkles, lemon juice, and brandy until well blended. Add this mixture to vegetables and crab and blend in.

Spread crab mixture equally over fillets. Sprinkle each with parsley, salt, and freshly ground pepper.

Fold heart in half over fish. Fold edges over a couple of times to seal. Place parchment packages on a rimmed baking sheet, folded sides up. Bake about 10 minutes, or until paper is browned. To serve, cut a large X on top of each package and pull paper back to let the wonderful aroma escape.

Each serving provides:

192	Calories	3 g	Carbohydrates
31 g	Protein	356 mg	Sodium
4 g	Fat	65 mg	Cholesterol
0 g	Dietary Fiber		

Pastry-Wrapped Fish with Mustard Sauce

What a wonderful party dish this makes! You can make one large pastry package to serve several people or you can make individual packages. Try tying each individual package for that special dinner with a whole chive so that they look like presents.

Because you are wrapping the fish in pastry it is very important to make sure that the fish is blotted dry. If you are using frozen fish, thaw it overnight in the refrigerator on paper towels, changing the towels a couple of times to soak up all the liquid.

Makes about 1-1/4 cups sauce

Pastry-wrapped fish:

6	slices orange roughy, sole, or red snapper (1-1/2 pounds total)
	juice of 1 lemon
1	tablespoon minced fresh dill
1	10-ounce package frozen chopped spinach, cooked and drained
1/3	cup crumbled feta
	butter-flavored vegetable oil spray
1/2	cup sliced mushrooms
1/4	cup sliced green onions
6	cloves garlic, minced
2	egg whites
1/2	teaspoon salt
1	teaspoon pepper
10	sheets phyllo dough (available frozen at many supermarkets)
	a sprinkling of dried parsley

Mustard sauce:

1	tablespoon minced shallots
2	cloves garlic, minced
1/4	cup white wine
1/2	cup fatfree sour cream
2/3	cup lite evaporated milk
	juice of 1 lemon mixed with 2 teaspoons cornstarch
1	tablespoon minced fresh dill
2	teaspoons dry mustard
	lemon pepper to taste
	salt to taste

Preheat oven to 425°.

Rub fish with lemon juice and fresh dill. Let sit for 20 minutes.

Squeeze cooked spinach to remove extra liquid. Put into a bowl and toss with feta. Set aside.

In a nonstick pan sprayed with butter-flavored vegetable oil spray, sauté the mushrooms, green onions and garlic until all liquid from the mushrooms has evaporated. Mix into the spinach-feta mixture. Stir in the egg whites, salt, and pepper. Refrigerate this filling for at least 1 hour.

Take a rimmed cookie sheet, line it with parchment paper, and put a piece of phyllo dough on the paper. Spray the dough with the vegetable oil spray. Lay another piece of phyllo on top of the first piece and spray with vegetable oil spray again. Repeat until you have 5 sheets of phyllo. (This makes 1 large package of fish that serves several people.) Lay two pieces of fish in the center of the pastry close to and parallel to one another. Lay the third piece close to and perpendicular to the others. Spread the cold spinach mixture over the fish. Now layer the last three pieces of fish over the filling the same way you layered the first three.

Do the same layering and spraying with 5 sheets of the phyllo dough as you did in the beginning, but this time put them on top of the fish. When you have laid down the last sheet of phyllo, fold the edges of the top sheets under the first stack of phyllo, so that you make a neat, tight package. Spray the top once more with the butter-flavored vegetable oil spray. Sprinkle with dried parsley. Bake for 25 to 30 minutes or until pastry is beautifully browned. Serve over a swirl of Mustard Sauce.

To prepare sauce: Put shallots, garlic, and wine into a small saucepan and cook until wine is reduced to 1 tablespoon. Remove from heat and stir in rest of sauce ingredients. Blend well and carefully warm until slightly thickened.

Each serving provides:

264	Calories	20 g	Carbohydrates
20 g	Protein	441 mg	Sodium
11 g	Fat	25 mg	Cholesterol
1 g	Dietary Fiber		

Italian Fish

Nothing tastes better on a cold night than this Italian Fish with a bottle of red wine and crusty french bread.

Makes 6 servings

2	pounds halibut, sea bass, or cod
1/2	cup sliced mushrooms
3	shallots, minced
4	cloves garlic, minced
2	tablespoons minced celery
1/4	cup chopped green bell pepper
2	teaspoons olive oil
1	cup diced fresh tomato sprinkled with 1 teaspoon sugar
2	tablespoons tomato puree
1/2	cup white wine
1/2	cup clam juice
1/4	cup slivered fresh basil
1/4	cup chopped fresh parsley
	salt and freshly ground pepper to taste
2	tablespoons grated Parmesan cheese (optional)

Cut fish into 2-inch strips and set aside.

Sauté mushrooms, shallots, garlic, celery, and bell pepper in a nonstick pan with the olive oil until vegetables begin to soften. Add tomato and cook 1 minute. Add tomato puree, wine, clam juice, basil, parsley, salt, and pepper. Cook until flavors combine, about 5 minutes.

Add fish, cover, and cook 5 to 10 minutes, depending on thickness of fish. Test by cutting open at thickest part. Flesh should be opaque but not dry. Sprinkle with Parmesan cheese if desired. This is delicious served over pasta.

Each serving provides:

217	Calories	5 g	Carbohydrates
32 g	Protein	154 mg	Sodium
5 g	Fat	48 mg	Cholesterol
1 g	Dietary Fiber		

Grilled Trout with Cucumber Sauce

If you do not own a grill basket, take a piece of heavy foil and poke some holes in it. Be careful when you turn the fish.

Makes 4 servings

Cucumber sauce:

1/2	cucumber, seeded and peeled
1/2	cup fatfree sour cream
2	tablespoons reduced-calorie mayonnaise
1	tablespoon fresh dill
1	tablespoon lemon juice
	freshly ground pepper and salt to taste

Grilling ingredients:

2	trout, opened flat (1 pound fish total, after cleaning and removing heads)
4	cloves garlic, minced
2	shallots, minced
1	teaspoon butter
1	tablespoon minced fresh dill
1	teaspoon dried marjoram
	juice of one lemon
2	teaspoons Worcestershire sauce
	vegetable oil spray

To prepare sauce: Grate cucumber, sprinkle with salt, and let drain 15 minutes. Rinse and squeeze dry. Mix cucumber with remaining sauce ingredients and blend well. Chill. Makes about 1 cup sauce.

Lay trout in a flat dish. Sauté the garlic and shallots in butter until they just are beginning to brown. Mix the garlic and shallots with the dill, marjoram, lemon juice, and Worcestershire sauce and rub on both sides of the trout.

Spray a grill basket with vegetable oil spray and lay fish in basket. Grill over hot coals for about 6 minutes. Turn and grill other side for 4 to 6 minutes or until fish flakes. Serve with Cucumber Sauce.

Each serving provides:

236	Calories	7 g	Carbohydrates
26 g	Protein	160 mg	Sodium
11 g	Fat	71 mg	Cholesterol
0 g	Dietary Fiber		

Grilled Orange Roughy in Orange Sauce

The orange sauce is good with any white-fleshed fish.

Makes 4 servings

1	pound orange roughy fillets
	vegetable oil spray
	salt and pepper
3	cloves garlic, minced
1	shallot, minced
2	teaspoons minced cilantro
2	teaspoons butter
1/2	cup orange juice
1	tablespoon triple sec
2	tablespoons fatfree sour cream

Spray grill or fish basket with vegetable oil spray. Season fish with salt and pepper. Grill orange roughy about 3 to 4 minutes each side per 1/2-inch thickness.

While fish is grilling, slowly sauté garlic, shallot, and cilantro in butter for 5 minutes. Add orange juice, triple sec, and sour cream. Cook 1 more minute, blending well. When fish is done spoon 2 tablespoons sauce over each fillet.

Each serving provides:

195	Calories	6 g	Carbohydrates
18 g	Protein	97 mg	Sodium
10 g	Fat	28 mg	Cholesterol
0 g	Dietary Fiber		

Grilled Fish with Mango Salsa

The Mango Salsa is also wonderful served alongside grilled chicken.

Makes 4 servings

1	tablespoon walnut oil
3	cloves garlic, chopped
1/4	cup thinly sliced green onion
1	tablespoon thinly sliced fresh basil
1	tablespoon thinly sliced fresh mint
1/2	teaspoon dill seed
1	teaspoon celery salt
1	cup finely diced mango
2	tablespoons plum wine
2	teaspoons sugar
1	tablespoon berry vinegar (raspberry, blueberry, or strawberry)
3	drops chili oil
	salt
1	pound fish fillets (such as sole, red snapper, or orange roughy)
	juice of 1 lemon
	vegetable oil spray
	pepper

To prepare the salsa: Sauté the garlic and green onion in the walnut oil. Add basil, mint, dill seed, and celery salt. Mix well. Add mango, wine, sugar, vinegar, and chili oil. Cook until mango softens. Season with salt to taste.

Spray grill or fish basket with vegetable oil spray. Rub fish with lemon juice and season with salt and pepper. Grill about 3 to 4 minutes each side or until fish flakes. Serve with 1 to 2 tablespoons salsa per serving.

Each serving provides:

189	Calories	12 g	Carbohydrates
22 g	Protein	256 mg	Sodium
5 g	Fat	54 mg	Cholesterol
1 g	Dietary Fiber		

Poached Salmon Steaks with Creamy Cucumber-Dill Sauce

This salmon is good eaten without the sauce, and the sauce is also delicious on broiled or grilled fish.

Makes 4 servings

Poached salmon steaks:
4   salmon steaks (about 5 ounces each)
4   thin lemon slices
        fresh dill, minced
4   cloves garlic, minced
        salt and freshly ground pepper to taste
2   tablespoons Worcestershire sauce
2   tablespoons lemon juice
2   tablespoons white wine
1   tablespoon capers
1   tablespoon tomato paste

Cucumber-dill sauce:
1   tablespoon grated seeded cucumber
1   tablespoon chopped seeded tomato
1   clove garlic, chopped
1/2   teaspoon minced fresh dill
2   tablespoons fatfree sour cream
1   tablespoon reduced-calorie mayonnaise
        salt and freshly ground pepper to taste

Preheat oven to 375°.

Put each salmon steak on a square of foil that will easily encase the salmon. On each steak put a lemon slice, some fresh dill, and minced garlic. Sprinkle each with a little salt and freshly ground pepper.

Mix the Worcestershire sauce, lemon juice, wine, capers, and tomato paste, until well blended. Spoon 2 tablespoons over each steak and roll foil up tightly, gathering the foil on top so no liquid escapes. Put the foil packets on a rimmed cookie sheet and bake for 15 to 20 minutes, or until fish flakes.

Blend all sauce ingredients and put a small teaspoon on each steak.

Each serving provides:			
218	Calories	6 g	Carbohydrates
26 g	Protein	253 mg	Sodium
9 g	Fat	70 mg	Cholesterol
0 g	Dietary Fiber		

Crab Puff Bake

Makes 8 servings

2	cups cooked crabmeat, fresh or canned
	juice of 1 lemon
1/3	cup sliced green onion
1	cup sliced mushrooms
1	celery stalk, minced
1	hot red chili pepper, minced
	vegetable oil spray
3	cups diced bread (crust removed before dicing)
1	teaspoon dried summer savory
1	teaspoon dried dill
	salt and cayenne pepper to taste
1	head garlic, roasted (see Basics) and squeezed into a cup
1	tablespoon Dijon mustard
1/4	cup fatfree cream cheese
1-1/2	cups lite evaporated milk
1/4	cup dry sherry
4	egg whites
2	tablespoons grated Parmesan cheese

Preheat oven to 350°.

If you are using canned crab, drain, then put crabmeat into a bowl. Mix with lemon juice and set aside. Sauté green onion, mushrooms, celery, and red chili pepper in vegetable oil spray until onion is soft. Add to crab.

Mix in bread cubes, summer savory, dill, salt, and cayenne.

Whisk the roasted garlic, mustard, cream cheese, evaporated milk, and sherry together and gently mix into crab.

Beat egg whites until stiff and fold into crab. Put into a baking dish sprayed with vegetable oil spray and bake, covered, for 40 minutes. Sprinkle with Parmesan cheese and bake uncovered, 10 minutes more or until lightly browned.

Each serving provides:

186	Calories	19 g	Carbohydrates
17 g	Protein	425 mg	Sodium
3 g	Fat	49 mg	Cholesterol
1 g	Dietary Fiber		

Shrimp and Garlic

Makes 6 servings

1-1/2 pounds large shrimp, shelled and deveined
2   teaspoons cornstarch mixed with 1 tablespoon water
       vegetable oil spray
1   tablespoon virgin olive oil
8   cloves garlic, minced
       juice of 1 lemon
1/2   small green bell pepper, julienned
1/2   cup vermouth
1/4   cup clam juice
2   tablespoons minced parsley
       salt and pepper to taste

Prepare shrimp by tossing with cornstarch mixture and set aside.

Spray a small nonstick pan with vegetable oil spray and then add olive oil. Add garlic to pan and cook very slowly over low heat for about 15 minutes. This is the most important part of the recipe, so take your time. Do not let the garlic burn.

Add shrimp and cook until shrimp are almost pink. Sprinkle on lemon juice, bell pepper, vermouth, and clam juice. Turn up heat slightly and continue cooking until shrimp are completely pink. Remove shrimp and bell pepper and let sauce cook 2 more minutes. Return shrimp and bell pepper to pan and stir to coat them completely with sauce. Sprinkle with parsley, and season with salt and pepper to taste.

Each serving provides:

152	Calories	4 g	Carbohydrates
19 g	Protein	160 mg	Sodium
4 g	Fat	140 mg	Cholesterol
0 g	Dietary Fiber		

Hawaiian Shrimp

This scrumptious combination of ingredients makes a striking presentation.

Makes 4 servings

1	cup chopped fresh pineapple (cut into thin chunks)
1	pound large shrimp, shelled and deveined
	vegetable oil spray
2	teaspoons arrowroot
2	tablespoons soy sauce
1	tablespoon hoisin sauce
1/3	cup pineapple juice
1	teaspoon sesame oil
3	cloves garlic, minced
1	teaspoon grated fresh ginger
1/2	cup sliced green onion (cut into 1-inch lengths)
1/2	green bell pepper, diced into 1/2-inch squares
1/3	cup bamboo shoots
12	snow peas

Cut pineapple and set aside.

Sauté shrimp in vegetable oil spray in a nonstick pan until shrimp are pink. Remove shrimp.

Mix arrowroot, soy sauce, hoisin sauce, and pineapple juice. Blend well until arrowroot is mixed in. Set aside.

In a nonstick pan, sauté garlic, ginger, green onion, and bell pepper in the sesame oil until you can smell the garlic and ginger, about 2 minutes. Add the pineapple, bamboo shoots, snow peas, and arrowroot mixture and cook until sauce begins to thicken. Add shrimp and cook 2 more minutes and serve.

Each serving provides:			
170	Calories	15 g	Carbohydrates
21 g	Protein	782 mg	Sodium
3 g	Fat	140 mg	Cholesterol
1 g	Dietary Fiber		

Shellfish Stirfry

Makes 4 servings

1	tablespoon virgin olive oil
1/2	pound shrimp, shelled, deveined, and diced large
1/2	pound small scallops, cut in half
1/2	pound lobster meat, cut into small pieces
6	cloves garlic, minced
	olive oil spray
1/4	cup julienned carrot
1/4	cup julienned leek
1/4	cup julienned red bell pepper
1/4	cup julienned celery
3	tablespoons slivered sorrel
1	teaspoon dried thyme
1/4	cup white wine
1/4	cup clam juice
	juice of 1 lemon
	salt and freshly ground pepper to taste
	slivered sorrel for garnish

Stirfry the shrimp, scallops, lobster, and garlic with the olive oil in a nonstick pan until the shrimp are pink. Remove the shellfish and set aside. Spray pan with olive oil spray and add the julienned vegetables, sorrel, and thyme to the pan. Cook until vegetables begin to soften. Add the wine, clam juice, and lemon juice, and let cook 1 minute. Return shellfish to pan, season with salt and pepper, and let fish cook until hot. Sprinkle with a little fresh sorrel and serve.

Each serving provides:

216	Calories	7 g	Carbohydrates
31 g	Protein	388 mg	Sodium
5 g	Fat	130 mg	Cholesterol
1 g	Dietary Fiber		

Shrimp and Halibut Bake with Creamy Wine Sauce

You can substitute any white-fleshed fish for the halibut, just make sure you adjust the baking time if you use a thin fillet.

Makes 6 servings

Shrimp and halibut bake:

	vegetable oil spray
2	pounds halibut, cut into 1-inch chunks
1/2	pound shrimp, shelled and deveined
	lemon pepper
1	tablespoon minced fresh dill
3	cloves garlic, sliced very thin
2	tablespoons chopped green onion

Creamy wine sauce:

4	ounces fatfree cream cheese
2/3	cup nonfat milk
1/4	cup fatfree sour cream
1/3	cup white wine
1/3	cup clam juice
1	tablespoon lemon juice
1	teaspoon butter sprinkles
	salt, pepper, and hot sauce to taste
1	tablespoon arrowroot mixed with 2 tablespoons white wine
3	tablespoons grated Parmesan cheese

Preheat oven to 350°.

Spray a baking dish with vegetable oil spray. Lay halibut and shrimp in pan. Sprinkle with some lemon pepper and fresh dill. Sauté garlic and green onion in a nonstick pan sprayed with vegetable oil spray until onions are soft. Sprinkle onion and garlic over fish.

Blend first 6 sauce ingredients and warm until cream cheese is blended. Add butter sprinkles, salt, pepper, and hot sauce and stir. Add arrowroot mixture and cook until sauce thickens. Pour sauce over fish and sprinkle with Parmesan cheese.

Bake for 15 minutes. Uncover and cook at least 5 more minutes or until Parmesan begins to brown and fish flakes.

Each serving provides:

271	Calories	6 g	Carbohydrates
45 g	Protein	388 mg	Sodium
5 g	Fat	101 mg	Cholesterol
0 g	Dietary Fiber		

Sole and Scallop Mousse with Yellow Pepper Sauce

A delicate mousse that takes a little time to make, it can be prepared ahead of time and baked at the last minute. This makes a beautiful first course.

Makes 6 servings

Mousse:

1/2	pound sole
1/2	pound scallops
1	head garlic, roasted (see Basics) and cloves squeezed into a bowl
3/4	cup lite evaporated milk
1/4	cup nonfat milk
1/2	cup sliced mushrooms
2	tablespoons grated onion
	vegetable oil spray
1/2	cup cooked, chopped spinach
2	egg whites
1	tablespoon chopped fresh lemon thyme
1/2	teaspoon salt
1/2	teaspoon white pepper

Yellow pepper sauce:

2	yellow bell peppers, roasted (see Basics)
1	teaspoon butter
1	leek, white part only, thinly sliced
1	tablespoon chopped fresh lemon thyme
1	tablespoon lemon juice
1/4	cup clam juice
1/2	cup nonfat milk
1	tablespoon arrowroot mixed with 3 tablespoons vermouth
	salt and white pepper to taste

Preheat oven to 350°.

Put sole, scallops, and garlic into a food processor fitted with the metal blade. Coarsely chop the fish. Slowly add the evaporated milk and nonfat milk. Process until mixture begins to puree.

Sauté the mushrooms and onion in a nonstick pan sprayed with vegetable oil spray until onions are soft. Add to processor bowl and process until well incorporated. Add spinach, egg whites, thyme, salt, and pepper. Process until well blended.

Spray 6 small ramekins with vegetable oil spray. Divide the fish mixture evenly among the ramekins. Smooth the top of each ramekin and cover with a piece of waxed paper the same size as the ramekin that has been sprayed with vegetable oil spray. Put the ramekins in a roasting pan and fill the pan with hot water halfway up the ramekins. Bake for 25 minutes. Remove from the oven and let sit a few minutes.

To prepare sauce: Put peppers in a food processor fitted with the metal blade and puree. Sauté the leek and lemon thyme in the butter and then add to the peppers. Puree again. Put the mixture into a saucepan and add lemon juice, clam juice, and milk. Heat and blend well. Add arrowroot mixture and blend until mixture thickens. Season with salt and pepper.

Put 2 tablespoons sauce on each plate. Remove the waxed paper from the ramekins, and turn the mousse out onto the plates. Garnish with some fresh lemon thyme.

Each serving provides:			
174	Calories	16 g	Carbohydrates
20 g	Protein	412 mg	Sodium
3 g	Fat	38 mg	Cholesterol
1 g	Dietary Fiber		

Grilled Lemon Chicken with Lemony Sauce

Chicken and Bean Bake

Chicken–Black Bean Burritos with
Sour Cream–Tomato Sauce

Chicken Smothered in Garlic

Chicken in Wine

Chicken Stirfry

Sweet and Sour Chicken

Chinese Chicken

Stuffed Chicken Breasts

Chicken and Dumplings

Chicken and Potatoes

Cornish Hens with Bell Peppers

Lemon-Grilled Cornish Hens

Stuffed Turkey Breast with Wine Sauce

Grilled Turkey Breast

Turkey Stroganoff

6

Poultry

An american favorite, poultry is loaded with protein and low in fat (when the skin is removed and it has not been deep fried). Many of us love fried chicken but there are plenty of new, delectable, and healthful ways to cook chicken other than frying it.

Poultry is inexpensive and can be quick and easy to cook. Unlike red meat, poultry must never be served rare, since this can be dangerous. Cooked poultry should be opaque and white in color when it is done.

Poultry is complemented by a multitude of flavors. It is wonderful added to pastas, vegetable stirfries, salads, soups, and casseroles. Feel free to add garlic, and lots of it, to any recipes you devise yourself, because garlic brings out the best in poultry.

Grilled Lemon Chicken with Lemony Sauce

I love the deep-fried lemon chicken from Chinese restaurants. We have cut the fat in this healthful dish, which has a wonderful lemony flavor.

Makes 8 servings

Grilled lemon chicken:

4	whole chicken breasts, halved, boned, and skinned
4	cloves garlic, minced
1/2	cup fresh lemon juice
1/4	cup tequila

Lemon sauce:

2	teaspoons butter
1/4	cup julienned leek
1/4	cup julienned carrot
1	tablespoon minced fresh parsley
1	tablespoon minced fresh tarragon
1	cup defatted chicken broth
1/4	cup lemon juice
2	tablespoons tequila
2	teaspoons lemon rind
2	teaspoons cornstarch mixed with 1 tablespoon water
	salt and pepper

Put chicken breasts into a bowl or casserole. Mix garlic, lemon juice, and tequila together. Pour over chicken and marinate for 30 minutes, turning the chicken a couple of times.

Grill chicken until done, about 5 to 6 minutes each side.

Meanwhile, make sauce. Sauté leek, carrot, and fresh herbs in butter. Add broth, lemon juice, tequila, and lemon rind and cook for 5 minutes. Thicken with cornstarch mixture and season with salt and pepper.

Each serving provides:

171	Calories	3 g	Carbohydrates
28 g	Protein	214 mg	Sodium
3 g	Fat	71 mg	Cholesterol
0 g	Dietary Fiber		

Chicken and Bean Bake

This dish is similar to a French cassoulet, but without the high-fat ingredients such as bacon and sausage. You won't miss them in this richly flavored casserole.

Makes 10 servings

1-1/2 pounds dried Great Northern or white beans, soaked in water overnight
       vegetable oil spray
4   whole chicken breasts, skinned, boned, and quartered
1   pound lean lamb, cut into small pieces
1-1/2 teaspoons smoke flavoring
1   tablespoon olive oil
2   large onions, diced small
8   cloves garlic, thinly sliced
4   carrots, peeled and sliced
4   celery stalks with leaves, chopped
1-1/2 teaspoons pepper
1   teaspoon each dried thyme, marjoram, sage, and mint
2   bay leaves
3   cups defatted chicken broth
1/2   cup vermouth
1   29-ounce can tomato sauce
       chopped fresh parsley for garnish

Preheat oven to 350°.

Drain beans after soaking. Brown the chicken in a nonstick pan sprayed with vegetable oil spray. Remove chicken and brown the lamb. Remove lamb. Sprinkle chicken and lamb with smoke flavoring and refrigerate until needed, keeping the meats separate, because we add them at different times.

In a large Dutch oven, sauté the onions and garlic in the olive oil. When onions become soft, add carrots, celery, pepper, herbs, broth, vermouth, and tomato sauce. Add the beans and bring to a boil.

Cover and bake for 1 hour. Add lamb and bake 30 more minutes. Add chicken and bake an additional 40 minutes, until chicken is done. Uncover, and bake 10 more minutes. Sprinkle with parsley and serve. You can add more broth or vermouth if needed while cooking.

Each serving provides:

489	Calories	59 g	Carbohydrates
49 g	Protein	922 mg	Sodium
7 g	Fat	85 mg	Cholesterol
30 g	Dietary Fiber		

Chicken–Black Bean Burritos with Sour Cream–Tomato Sauce

These burritos have no cheese or guacamole, use fatfree sour cream, and taste fantastic.

Makes about 8 burritos

Burritos:

	vegetable oil spray
3	half chicken breasts, skinned, boned, and diced
1	onion, chopped
1	head garlic, blanched (see Basics) and chopped
1/4	cup chopped red bell pepper
1/4	cup chopped yellow bell pepper
1	carrot, shredded
2	cups cooked black beans (see Basics)
	salt and cumin to taste
	juice of 1 lime
1	cup uncooked rice
2-1/2	cups defatted chicken broth
1	tablespoon tomato paste
8	large flour tortillas

Sauce:

1	cup fatfree sour cream
1	large fresh tomato, chopped
1	tablespoon minced cilantro
1	tablespoon thinly sliced green onion
	salt and pepper to taste

Spray a nonstick pan with vegetable oil spray and sauté chicken until no longer pink. Remove chicken, spray with vegetable oil spray again, and add onion, garlic, bell pepper, and carrot. Cook until vegetables begin to soften. Put vegetables and chicken into a saucepan and add beans, salt, cumin, lime juice, and rice. Mix chicken broth with tomato paste and add to pan. Mix well, cover, and cook until rice is done, about 20 to 25 minutes. Cool slightly.

Make sauce by combining all sauce ingredients.

To assemble burritos: Spoon chicken-bean mixture down the center of a softened flour tortilla. Tuck in ends and roll up. I like to microwave the burritos for 2 minutes (or steam if you do not have a microwave) and then top each burrito with a tablespoon of sauce.

Each serving provides:			
559	Calories	82 g	Carbohydrates
37 g	Protein	807 mg	Sodium
8 g	Fat	51 mg	Cholesterol
5 g	Dietary Fiber		

Chicken Smothered in Garlic

Serve this chicken with french bread so you can spread the cooked garlic on the bread. It's scrumptious!

Makes 8 servings

4   whole chicken breasts, split, skinned, and boned
       olive oil spray
2   heads of garlic, blanched (see Basics)
2   cups chopped fresh tomatoes
1/2   cup white wine
1/2   cup defatted chicken broth
2   tablespoons minced fresh tarragon
1/2   teaspoon dried marjoram
       salt and freshly ground pepper to taste
       fresh parsley for garnish

Preheat oven to 350°.

Sauté chicken breasts in a nonstick pan using olive oil spray. Lay chicken breasts in a single layer in a baking pan. Sprinkle the garlic cloves over the breasts. Add tomatoes, wine, broth, tarragon, and marjoram. Season with salt and pepper. Cover pan tightly and bake for 45 to 50 minutes.

Each serving provides:

170	Calories	8 g	Carbohydrates
29 g	Protein	146 mg	Sodium
2 g	Fat	68 mg	Cholesterol
1 g	Dietary Fiber		

Chicken in Wine

Makes 6 servings

6   half chicken breasts, skinned and boned
1/2   cup flour
1/2   teaspoon *each* salt and pepper
1   tablespoon *each* dried parsley and tarragon
4   cloves garlic, minced
1   teaspoon *each* butter and olive oil
1/2   cup diced green onion
1   cup dry white wine
          juice of 1 lemon
1/2   cup lite evaporated milk
1 to 3 tablespoons capers
          salt and freshly ground pepper to taste

Pound breasts between two pieces of waxed paper until nice and thin. Mix flour, salt, pepper, parsley, and tarragon. Rinse breasts in water and then dip into flour mixture. Sauté chicken and garlic in butter-oil mixture until golden and chicken has cooked through.

Meanwhile, put green onion and wine into a small saucepan and boil until liquid has reduced by half. Stir in lemon juice and evaporated milk. Add capers to taste. Season with salt and freshly ground pepper. Cook 2 minutes until well blended.

Pour sauce over chicken and serve.

Each serving provides:

209	Calories	13 g	Carbohydrates
30 g	Protein	365 mg	Sodium
3 g	Fat	74 mg	Cholesterol
1 g	Dietary Fiber		

Chicken Stirfry

Makes 6 servings

1	pound chicken breasts, skinned, boned, and diced
4	teaspoons cornstarch
2	teaspoons sesame oil
	vegetable oil spray
1/3	cup lite soy sauce
2	tablespoons oyster sauce
2	tablespoons rice vinegar
3/4	teaspoon sugar
1/3	cup defatted chicken broth
1/3	cup water
4	cloves garlic, chopped
1	medium onion, thinly sliced
2-1/2	cups broccoli flowerets
3	baby bok choy, white part only, cut into chunks
3/4	cup diagonally sliced carrot

Toss diced chicken in 1 tablespoon water mixed with 2 teaspoons of the cornstarch. Let sit while you chop the vegetables.

In a nonstick pan, put 1 teaspoon sesame oil. Spray pan with some vegetable oil spray. Sauté half the chicken until almost done. Remove from pan and repeat with rest of chicken. Set chicken aside.

Mix soy sauce, oyster sauce, vinegar, and sugar in a small dish. In another small dish mix broth, 1/3 cup water, and remaining 2 teaspoons cornstarch. Set aside.

Spray a nonstick pan with vegetable oil spray and stirfry garlic and onion until garlic begins to brown. Add vegetables and 2 to 3 tablespoons water. Cover pan and cook vegetables 2 minutes. Add the chicken and the soy mixture, cover, and cook 2 more minutes. Stir the cornstarch mixture and add to stirfry. Toss well and cook for 2 to 3 minutes or until thickened. Serve over plain rice.

Each serving provides:

168	Calories	13 g	Carbohydrates
22 g	Protein	917 mg	Sodium
3 g	Fat	44 mg	Cholesterol
3 g	Dietary Fiber		

Sweet and Sour Chicken

Makes 6 servings

6	half chicken breasts, skinned, boned, and diced large
4	cloves garlic, chopped
	sesame oil spray (see Basics)
1/4	cup brown sugar
1/4	cup red wine vinegar mixed with 3 teaspoons cornstarch
1/4	cup defatted chicken broth
1/2	cup pineapple chunks with juice
1	tablespoon soy sauce
1/2	teaspoon grated fresh ginger
1/4	cup diced green bell pepper
1/4	cup bamboo shoots
1/4	cup chopped green onion

Mix the chicken with the garlic and let marinate for 15 minutes.

Sauté the chicken in a pan sprayed with sesame oil spray until lightly browned. Remove the chicken and add remaining ingredients to the pan. Mix well and cook until the sauce begins to thicken. Add chicken and cook 2 minutes to blend flavors.

Each serving provides:

194	Calories	16 g	Carbohydrates
28 g	Protein	294 mg	Sodium
2 g	Fat	69 mg	Cholesterol
0 g	Dietary Fiber		

Chinese Chicken

The lemongrass, bamboo shoots, black bean sauce, and black sesame seeds can be found in any Oriental market and some specialty grocery stores. I like serving this colorful dish over white rice on black plates.

Makes 6 servings

3	half chicken breasts, boned, skinned, and diced
1	teaspoon cornstarch mixed with 2 tablespoons water
5	cloves garlic, minced
2	tablespoons minced lemongrass
	sesame oil spray (see Basics)
1/4	cup slivered red bell pepper
1/4	cup slivered green bell pepper
1/3	cup sliced mushrooms
1/3	cup bamboo shoots
1	celery stalk, thinly sliced
1/2	cup snow peas
1/3	cup sliced carrot
2	green onions, sliced
1	teaspoon grated fresh ginger
2	tablespoons soy sauce
1/3	cup defatted chicken broth
2	tablespoons oyster sauce
1	tablespoon black bean sauce
	chili paste to taste (I like it hot)
	black sesame seeds

Mix diced chicken with cornstarch-water mixture. Let sit while you slice the vegetables.

Sauté chicken, garlic, and lemongrass in sesame oil spray until chicken is done. Remove chicken and to same pan add bell peppers, mushrooms, bamboo shoots, celery, snow peas, and carrot. Add 2 tablespoons water to the pan, cover, and cook 2 to 3 minutes. Add remaining ingredients (except black sesame seeds). Mix well and add chicken. Cook 3 to 5 minutes to blend flavors and until vegetables are done to the tenderness you desire. Sprinkle with a few black sesame seeds and serve immediately.

Each serving provides:

180	Calories	7 g	Carbohydrates
30 g	Protein	725 mg	Sodium
3 g	Fat	68 mg	Cholesterol
1 g	Dietary Fiber		

Stuffed Chicken Breasts

These chicken breasts have a beautiful mosaic pattern when they are sliced and can be served hot or cold. They can also be served as appetizers or as part of a composed salad. Baking parchment can be found in specialty food stores.

Makes 6 main-dish servings

6	half chicken breasts, boned and skinned
1/2	cup lowfat ricotta cheese
1	egg white
3	cloves garlic, minced
1/2	teaspoon pepper
1/2	teaspoon dried oregano
	vegetable seasoning (such as Vegit®)
1	tablespoon minced fresh cilantro
6	large spinach leaves, washed and dried
6	carrots, cut into 1/4-inch wide, 3-inch long sticks
6	celery stalks, cut into 1/4-inch wide, 3-inch long sticks
1/4	pound deli ham, cut into 1/4-inch wide, 3-inch long sticks
3/4	cup pureed salsa
1	cup bread crumbs

Preheat oven to 375°.

Prepare chicken breasts by flattening between two pieces of waxed paper.

In a bowl mix the ricotta, egg white, garlic, pepper, oregano, vegetable seasoning, and cilantro.

Take one flattened chicken breast and lay a spinach leaf on the breast. Spread the spinach with 1-1/2 to 2 tablespoons of the cheese mixture. Lay a piece of carrot, celery, and ham on the cheese. Sprinkle with a little vegetable seasoning. Carefully roll up breasts. Roll breasts in salsa and then in the bread crumbs. Lay seam side down on a cookie sheet lined with parchment paper.

Continue until all breasts are done. Bake for 30 to 40 minutes.

Each serving provides:

309	Calories	26 g	Carbohydrates
38 g	Protein	758 mg	Sodium
6 g	Fat	82 mg	Cholesterol
4 g	Dietary Fiber		

Chicken and Dumplings

Chicken and Dumplings is an old-time favorite. We have no reason to yearn for the wonderful but heavy recipes of yesterday with delicious lowfat versions such as this.

Makes 8 servings

Chicken and broth:

1/2	cup flour
1/2	teaspoon pepper
4	whole chicken breasts, skinned and cut in quarters
	vegetable oil spray
1	16-ounce can pearl onions, drained
6	cloves garlic, chopped
4	cups defatted chicken broth
1/2	cup vermouth
1	teaspoon *each* dried thyme, parsley, basil, and sage
2	carrots, thickly sliced
1	cup sliced mushrooms
1/2	cup thickly sliced celery
2	potatoes, peeled and diced large
	salt and pepper to taste

Dumplings

1-1/2	cups flour
1	teaspoon *each* pepper, thyme, and sage
1-1/2	teaspoons baking powder
2	tablespoons fatfree cream cheese
3	cloves garlic, minced
1	tablespoon minced fresh parsley
1/4	cup egg substitute
1	cup nonfat milk

Preheat oven to 350°.

Mix 1/2 cup flour with 1/2 teaspoon pepper. Dredge chicken in flour mixture. Sauté in a nonstick pan sprayed with vegetable oil spray. When all chicken has browned, set aside. In same nonstick pan, sauté pearl onions and garlic until garlic begins to turn color. Put onions, garlic, and chicken in an ovenproof Dutch oven. Add broth, vermouth, and dried herbs. Heat on top of stove until it comes to a boil. Cover and bake for 15 minutes. Add carrots, mush-

continued on next page

rooms, celery, and potatoes and cook 20 more minutes. Remove
from oven and assemble dumplings.

To assemble dumplings: Mix flour, pepper, thyme, sage, and
baking powder. Cut the cream cheese into the flour mixture with a
pastry blender or fork. Add garlic, parsley, egg substitute, and milk.
Don't overmix, just blend so all ingredients are wet.

Put Dutch oven on top of stove and drop tablespoons of
dumpling mixture on top of the chicken. Cover, and simmer for 20
minutes. Do not remove lid once dumplings have been added. Salt
and pepper to taste before serving.

Each serving provides:

339	Calories	40 g	Carbohydrates
36 g	Protein	941 mg	Sodium
3 g	Fat	70 mg	Cholesterol
3 g	Dietary Fiber		

Chicken and Potatoes

Makes 6 servings

3	whole chicken breasts, halved and skinned
1/3	cup flour mixed with 1/4 teaspoon *each* salt and pepper
	vegetable oil spray
1	tablespoon butter
3	potatoes, cut in sixths
1/2	cup sliced green onion
6	cloves garlic, chopped
2	tablespoons flour
1-1/2	cups white wine
2	cups defatted chicken broth
1/3	cup chopped fresh basil
1/4	cup chopped fresh parsley
2	teaspoons pepper
1	14-ounce can artichoke hearts (not marinated)
	chopped fresh parsley for garnish

Dip chicken in flour, salt, and pepper mixture. Sauté in a non-stick pan that has been sprayed with vegetable oil spray until chicken has browned. Remove chicken and sauté potatoes, green onion, and garlic in butter for 5 minutes. Add 2 tablespoons flour and cook until no white from the flour shows. Stir in the wine and broth and bring to a simmer, stirring until smooth. Add basil, parsley, and 2 teaspoons pepper. Return chicken to pan and add artichoke hearts. Simmer, covered, for 40 to 50 minutes. Serve sprinkled with fresh parsley.

Each serving provides:

285	Calories	28 g	Carbohydrates
33 g	Protein	548 mg	Sodium
4 g	Fat	74 mg	Cholesterol
4 g	Dietary Fiber		

Cornish Hens with Bell Peppers

This dish can be made with chicken just as easily but the little hen halves are very pretty.

Makes 4 servings

2   cornish hens, cut in half and skinned
1   tablespoon virgin olive oil
8   cloves garlic, thinly sliced
1/2   *each* red and green bell peppers, julienned
1/2   small onion, slivered
1-1/2 to 2 cups defatted chicken broth
3   plum tomatoes, peeled and diced
1/3   cup chopped fresh basil
1   tablespoon chopped fresh parsley
2/3   cup white wine
1   cup lite evaporated milk
     salt and pepper to taste
1   tablespoon freshly grated Parmesan cheese

Sauté hens in olive oil until nicely browned. Remove hens and put garlic, peppers, and onion in pan. Add 2 tablespoons of the chicken broth and cook until broth has evaporated. Add tomatoes, basil, parsley, 1-1/2 cups broth, and wine. Return hens to pan. Simmer, covered, for 40 minutes. Add more broth if necessary, and turn hens once or twice during cooking. Remove cover and add evaporated milk. Season with salt and pepper. Warm very carefully once the milk has been added. Remove to a serving dish and sprinkle with grated Parmesan cheese.

Each serving provides:			
302	Calories	14 g	Carbohydrates
27 g	Protein	590 mg	Sodium
13 g	Fat	68 mg	Cholesterol
1 g	Dietary Fiber		

Lemon-Grilled Cornish Hens

In this recipe I cook the hens with their skin on and then remove it before eating them. This marinade will give you lots of great flavor, even without the skin.

Makes 4 servings

4	small cornish hens
1	cup *fresh* lemon juice (please don't use bottled)
1/4	cup minced fresh lemon thyme
4	tablespoons minced garlic
1	shallot, minced
1/4	cup tequila
2	teaspoons cracked black pepper
1-1/2	teaspoons sea salt
	thin lemon slices for garnish

Cut cornish hens down the back and open them up flat by pressing down on the breast bone. Stick a brochette prong through each hen from wing to wing so the hens will lay flat when cooking.

Mix the lemon juice, thyme, garlic, shallot, and tequila together. Crush the cracked pepper and sea salt together and rub into the cornish hens. Lay hens in a pan and pour lemon mixture over all. Cover and marinate in the refrigerator for at least 2 hours. Grill for 40 minutes. Serve garnished with thinly sliced lemon.

Each serving provides:

334	Calories	5 g	Carbohydrates
31 g	Protein	644 mg	Sodium
15 g	Fat	97 mg	Cholesterol
0 g	Dietary Fiber		

Stuffed Turkey Breast with Wine Sauce

A marvelous party dish, this can be prepared ahead of time. If you do so, make sure to take it out of the refrigerator at least 30 minutes before baking so that the turkey breast is completely hot when the phyllo is golden brown. The sauce can be made ahead of time as well. Baking parchment can be found in specialty food stores.

Makes 10 servings

Stuffed turkey breast:

1	4-pound rolled turkey breast, thawed and flattened butter-flavored vegetable oil spray
3	tablespoons minced green onion
3	tablespoons minced red bell pepper
2	tablespoons minced celery
1	10-ounce package frozen spinach, cooked and drained
1	cup fatfree ricotta cheese
5	cloves garlic, minced for stuffing
2	tablespoons grated Parmesan cheese
1	egg white
1	teaspoon dried oregano
1/2	teaspoon dried sage
1	teaspoon dried tarragon
4	cloves garlic, minced for rubbing over turkey salt and pepper
7	sheets phyllo dough
1	egg white

Wine sauce:

2	cups defatted chicken broth
1	cup white wine
1	cup lite evaporated milk
2	teaspoons cornstarch mixed with 2 tablespoons water vegetable oil spray
1	tablespoon chopped green onion
1/4	cup sliced mushrooms
1/2	teaspoon salt
1/2	teaspoon white pepper

Preheat oven to 450°.

Unroll turkey breast and flatten. Lay some kitchen string under the turkey so that you can securely tie the breast when it has been stuffed.

Spray a nonstick pan with butter-flavored vegetable oil spray and sauté the green onion, bell pepper, and celery, until vegetables are soft. Remove from heat, and add spinach, ricotta cheese, 5 cloves minced garlic, Parmesan cheese, egg white, and dried herbs. Mix well. Spread the mixture evenly over the turkey. Roll the turkey up carefully and tie with string. Rub the breast with 4 cloves minced garlic and sprinkle with salt and pepper.

When you put the turkey breast in the oven immediately turn the oven down to 350°. Bake for 1-1/2 hours. Remove from oven and let cool completely. Refrigerate if you'll be serving this later in the day.

To assemble finished product: Lay a sheet of phyllo on a flat surface. Spray with butter-flavored vegetable oil spray. Continue layering the phyllo sheets and spraying with vegetable oil spray until you have a stack of 7 sheets. Remove the string and skin from the turkey. Pat dry. Lay the turkey on the phyllo. Brush the edges of the phyllo with egg white wash (1 egg white mixed with 1 tablespoon water). Carefully cover entire breast, ends and all, with phyllo, wrapping it like a package. Place seam side down on a baking pan lined with parchment paper.

Spray entire surface of package with vegetable oil spray. Bake in a 400° oven until phyllo is beautifully golden, about 20 to 30 minutes.

To prepare sauce: Combine broth, wine, and milk in heavy pot. Reduce to 1 cup by cooking slowly. Add cornstarch mixture and blend until mixture thickens and is smooth and velvety.

In a separate nonstick pan sprayed with vegetable oil spray, sauté green onion and mushrooms until tender. Add to sauce and season with salt and pepper. Makes 1-1/4 cups sauce.

Serve turkey with 2 tablespoons sauce per person.

Each serving provides:

310	Calories	13 g	Carbohydrates
52 g	Protein	554 mg	Sodium
4 g	Fat	117 mg	Cholesterol
1 g	Dietary Fiber		

Grilled Turkey Breast

This simple marinade is also outstanding on chicken, cornish hens, pork, or beef.

Makes 6 servings

2	pounds skinless, boneless turkey breast
3	cloves garlic, minced
	salt and pepper
1/2	cup defatted chicken broth
1/2	cup lite soy sauce
1/2	cup rice vinegar
1-1/2	teaspoons sugar
2	teaspoons cornstarch mixed with 2 tablespoons water

Rub turkey breast with garlic, salt, and pepper. Mix broth, soy sauce, and rice vinegar together in a pan and bring to a boil. Remove from heat and cool. Pour half the sauce over the turkey and let marinate 20 minutes. Take the other half of the sauce, add the sugar, reheat, and thicken with cornstarch mixture. Grill turkey breast using the thickened sauce to baste the turkey.

Each serving provides:

293	Calories	8 g	Carbohydrates
58 g	Protein	960 mg	Sodium
2 g	Fat	141 mg	Cholesterol
0 g	Dietary Fiber		

Turkey Stroganoff

The roasted garlic not only tastes wonderful but also thickens the sauce.
You can substitute chicken or lean beef for the turkey.

Makes 6 servings

1	pound turkey breast, boned, skinned, and thinly sliced
	butter-flavored vegetable oil spray
1/4	cup chopped green onion
1/2	cup sliced shiitake mushrooms
1/3	cup julienned carrot, parboiled
1	head garlic, roasted (see Basics)
1/4	cup defatted chicken broth
1	teaspoon Worcestershire sauce
1/2	teaspoon butter sprinkles
1/2	cup sherry
1/2	cup fatfree sour cream
	salt and pepper to taste
6	ounces dry noodles, cooked

Sauté turkey in a nonstick pan sprayed with butter-flavored vegetable oil spray. Remove turkey when cooked through. Sauté the green onion, mushrooms, and carrot in vegetable oil spray until mushrooms begin to get soft.

Squeeze out all roasted garlic and puree. To garlic add broth, Worcestershire sauce, butter sprinkles, and sherry. Mix until well blended. Add mixture to vegetables and cook 2 minutes. Turn heat down and gently stir in sour cream and season with salt and pepper. Cook 1 more minute. Stir in turkey and cook gently 2 more minutes. Serve over noodles.

Each serving provides:

265	Calories	29 g	Carbohydrates
25 g	Protein	154 mg	Sodium
2 g	Fat	74 mg	Cholesterol
1 g	Dietary Fiber		

Grilled Lamb with Pears and Mint

Veal Chops with Orange Sauce

Stirfried Veal with Asparagus

Beef and Garlic

Stuffed Eye of the Round with Leek Sauce

Grilled Beef and Peppers

Broccoli and Beef Stirfry

Jill's Spicy Chili

Spicy Beef

Beef in Creamy Mushroom Sauce

Pork Tenderloin in Fruit Sauce

Pork Tenderloin with Apples

Pork Tenderloin with Garlic and Rosemary

Pork Leg Roast with Garlicky Gravy

Pork Rolls with Apricot Sauce

7

Meat

Some of my favorite childhood memories are of incredible meals consisting of chops, stews, ribs, roasts, and steaks smothered in onions and mushrooms. How I loved the smell of a garlic-studded roast cooking, knowing it would be accompanied by Yorkshire pudding and delicious roasted potatoes. Well, those days are over and lifestyles and dining habits have changed.

Today we all realize that we should reduce the amount of red meat in our diet. However, meat can still be part of a healthful diet if eaten in moderation. The meat industry has helped by providing leaner, lighter cuts of meat. Serving sizes should be limited to about 3 ounces (cooked) and consumption cut to no more than twice a week. Many countries use meat almost like a garnish, and that is a reasonable way to think of it. When you stirfry or add fruit, vegetables, or pasta to meat, you have a healthful and filling meal that has used very little meat while fulfilling your yearning for a succulent meal.

Grilled Lamb with Pears and Mint

The spicy fruit sauce makes this lamb dish memorable.

Makes 12 servings

Grilled lamb:
1   3-pound boneless leg of lamb, all visible fat removed
6   cloves garlic, minced
      salt and pepper

Pear sauce:
2   firm pears, peeled, seeded, and sliced lengthwise into eighths
1   bunch of green onions, sliced diagonally
1/4 cup slivered fresh mint
3   cloves garlic, slivered
2   teaspoons butter
1   tablespoon sugar
2   tablespoons hoisin sauce
1   tablespoon oyster sauce
1   tablespoon soy sauce
1   teaspoon grated fresh ginger
1   cup defatted chicken broth
1/2 cup plum wine
2   teaspoons cornstarch mixed with 2 tablespoons water
      salt and pepper to taste

Rub the lamb with the minced garlic, salt, and pepper. Grill on hot coals about 15 minutes each side or until it reaches desired doneness.

Meanwhile, sauté the pears, green onions, mint, and slivered garlic in the butter for 3 minutes. Blend in the sugar, hoisin sauce, oyster sauce, soy sauce, ginger, broth, and wine. Cook 2 minutes. Blend in cornstarch mixture and cook until sauce thickens. Taste and season with salt and pepper. Serve over grilled lamb.

Each serving provides:			
221	Calories	10 g	Carbohydrates
25 g	Protein	380 mg	Sodium
8 g	Fat	77 mg	Cholesterol
1 g	Dietary Fiber		

Veal Chops with Orange Sauce

An 8-ounce chop will produce a 4-ounce serving, excluding the bone, when it is trimmed of all fat.

Makes 4 servings

Veal chops:

4	8-ounce veal chops, trimmed of all fat
4	cloves garlic, minced
	salt, pepper, and chopped fresh rosemary
1	tablespoon olive oil

Orange sauce:

1/4	cup defatted chicken broth
1/4	cup minced shallots
3	cloves garlic, minced
1	pound mushrooms, chopped
1/2	cup flour
1	cup *each* orange juice, water, chicken broth
1	tablespoon brown sugar
1	tablespoon granulated sugar
1	tablespoon chopped fresh rosemary
1	tablespoon chopped fresh parsley
1	tablespoon orange rind
2	tablespoons orange liqueur

Rub chops with 4 cloves minced garlic, salt, pepper, and fresh rosemary. Sauté chops in the olive oil in a very hot pan until nicely browned. Remove chops and add 1/4 cup chicken broth, shallots, 3 cloves minced garlic, and mushrooms to pan. Cook until all liquid has evaporated. Stir in flour and cook, stirring, until no more white flour shows. Whisk in 1 cup each orange juice, water, and broth. Cook until smooth. Add remaining ingredients and blend. Return chops to pan, cover, and simmer until chops are tender, about 25 to 35 minutes.

Each serving provides:			
459	Calories	37 g	Carbohydrates
44 g	Protein	413 mg	Sodium
15 g	Fat	142 mg	Cholesterol
2 g	Dietary Fiber		

Stirfried Veal with Asparagus

When asparagus shows up in the spring it's great in all kinds of dishes. I love to use the thin, crisp asparagus that comes to market in March in this recipe. Fish sauce is available in the Oriental section of many supermarkets.

Makes 6 servings

3/4	pound veal scallops, cut in 1/2-inch julienne strips
1	small onion, thinly sliced
4	cloves garlic, minced
1/2	teaspoon sesame oil
1	red bell pepper, julienned
1-1/2	pounds thin asparagus, cut diagonally into 1-inch slices
1	carrot, cut diagonally into thin slices
1/2	cup defatted beef broth
2	teaspoons chili paste
1/2	cup fish sauce
1	tablespoon catsup
2	tablespoons soy sauce
1	teaspoon grated fresh ginger
1/3	cup white wine
2	teaspoons sugar
2	teaspoons cornstarch mixed with 2 tablespoons water
	salt and pepper to taste

Sauté the veal, onion, and garlic in the sesame oil until meat is light pink. Add the bell pepper, asparagus, and carrot. Pour in 2 tablespoons of the beef broth and let cook 2 minutes. Add remaining ingredients, except for the cornstarch mixture, and blend well. Cook until vegetables are done. Stir in cornstarch mixture and cook until thickened. Taste and correct seasonings.

Each serving provides:			
192	Calories	16 g	Carbohydrates
20 g	Protein	499 mg	Sodium
5 g	Fat	44 mg	Cholesterol
2 g	Dietary Fiber		

Beef and Garlic

Makes 4 servings

1	pound beef sirloin, thinly sliced
6	cloves garlic, thinly sliced
	vegetable oil spray
2	green onions, sliced
1/2	pound bok choy, sliced
3	tablespoons lite soy sauce
1	tablespoon oyster sauce
1/3	cup defatted beef broth
1	tomato, peeled and cut into eighths
	salt and pepper to taste

Mix beef and garlic and let sit 10 minutes. Sauté beef and garlic in a nonstick pan sprayed with vegetable oil spray. When beef is done, remove. In the same pan, sauté green onions and bok choy until vegetables are tender. Return beef to pan and add soy sauce, oyster sauce, beef broth, and tomato and cook for 3 minutes. Season with salt and pepper to taste.

Each serving provides:

186	Calories	7 g	Carbohydrates
27 g	Protein	804 mg	Sodium
6 g	Fat	69 mg	Cholesterol
1 g	Dietary Fiber		

Stuffed Eye of the Round with Leek Sauce

A magnificent main course when company's coming.

Makes 12 servings

Stuffing:
1-1/2 cups sliced mushrooms
1/2   cup chopped fresh spinach
4   cloves garlic, chopped
1/4   cup sliced green onion
       vegetable oil spray
1   teaspoon vegetable seasoning (such as Vegit®)
3   tablespoons defatted beef broth
3   tablespoons brandy
       salt and freshly ground pepper to taste

Roast:
1   3-pound eye of the round roast
3   cloves garlic, minced
       thyme, salt, and pepper

Leek sauce:
1   tablespoon butter
2   leeks, white part only, thinly sliced
1/4   cup flour
1   cup defatted beef broth
3   tablespoons whiskey
1   tablespoon minced fresh parsley
1   teaspoon dried thyme
       salt and pepper to taste

Preheat oven to 450°.

To prepare the stuffing: Sauté mushrooms, spinach, 4 cloves chopped garlic, and green onion in a nonstick pan sprayed with vegetable oil spray for 5 minutes. Add vegetable seasoning, 3 tablespoons beef broth, and brandy and cook until liquid evaporates. Season to taste with salt and pepper and set aside.

Cut roast open lengthwise and make a pocket in the meat. Stuff the meat with the mushroom-spinach mixture. Gently roll and tie the meat with twine.

Rub the rolled meat with 3 cloves minced garlic, thyme, salt, and pepper. Set on a rack in a roasting pan and roast for 20 minutes.

continued on next page

Reduce heat to 375° and roast for 1 more hour or until desired doneness is reached.

To make sauce: Put butter in a nonstick pan and sauté leeks. When leeks are soft, add flour and cook until flour just begins to turn brown. Whisk in 1 cup beef broth, whiskey, thyme, and parsley. Add salt and pepper to taste. Cook until thickened and serve with roast.

Each serving provides:

235	Calories	6 g	Carbohydrates
23 g	Protein	163 mg	Sodium
12 g	Fat	62 mg	Cholesterol
0 g	Dietary Fiber		

Grilled Beef and Peppers

Leftovers are great cold—as a beautiful salad or as a sandwhich filling on a french roll.

Makes 6 servings

2	cloves garlic, minced for rubbing on meat
1	pound London broil
1	teaspoon *each* dried oregano, basil, and parsley
1/3	cup red wine vinegar
1	bay leaf
1	tablespoon Worcestershire sauce
1	tablespoon soy sauce
	juice of 1 lemon
1/4	cup Madeira
1/2	*each* red, yellow, and green bell peppers, diced
1/2	cup sliced mushrooms
1/2	onion, thinly sliced
3	cloves garlic, slivered to sauté with vegetables
1	tablespoon olive oil
1	beef bouillon cube mixed with 1/4 cup boiling water
2	tablespoons cornstarch mixed with 3 tablespoons water
	salt and pepper to taste

Rub minced garlic on London broil and put meat into a dish. Sprinkle meat with dried herbs. Mix together vinegar, bay leaf, Worcestershire sauce, soy sauce, lemon juice, and Madeira and pour over meat. Let marinate 20 minutes. Remove meat from marinade, reserving marinade, and grill until meat is done as you like it.

Sauté the bell peppers, mushrooms, onion, and slivered garlic in olive oil until vegetables are al dente. Stir in bouillon mixture and reserved meat marinade. Add cornstarch mixture and cook until sauce has thickened. Season with salt and pepper. Slice meat thin and serve with 2 tablespoons of sauce per serving.

Each serving provides:

196	Calories	9 g	Carbohydrates
16 g	Protein	392 mg	Sodium
9 g	Fat	38 mg	Cholesterol
1 g	Dietary Fiber		

Broccoli and Beef Stirfry

A hearty dish that uses very little meat.

Makes 8 servings

1	pound lean beef sirloin or fillet
4	cloves garlic, minced
1/3	cup soy sauce
2	tablespoons rice vinegar
1	teaspoon sugar
1	teaspoon beef soup base or 1 bouillon cube
1/3	cup water
3	teaspoons cornstarch
	vegetable oil spray
1	small yellow onion, thinly sliced
1/2	cup thinly sliced celery
1/2	cup thinly sliced carrot
3	cups broccoli flowerets
1/2	cup sugar snap peas

Partially freeze meat (about 3 hours) and slice very thin (about 1/8-inch thick) with slicing blade of food processor or a sharp knife. Let meat thaw completely. Mix minced garlic with meat and let sit while you slice vegetables.

Mix soy sauce, vinegar, sugar, soup base, water, and cornstarch together and set aside.

Spray a wok with vegetable oil spray and stirfry meat a quarter pound at a time until all meat is done. Remove meat. Spray wok with vegetable oil spray again and add onion. Stirfry a few minutes. Add celery, carrots, and broccoli. Add 2 tablespoons water, cover, and cook 2 minutes. Stir soy mixture again and add to wok. Cover and cook another 2 minutes. Add meat and peas and cook until vegetables are done. Serve with white rice.

Each serving provides:

119	Calories	9 g	Carbohydrates
15 g	Protein	842 mg	Sodium
3 g	Fat	35 mg	Cholesterol
2 g	Dietary Fiber		

Jill's Spicy Chili

Jill is a wonderful friend of mine and a truly great cook—as you'll see when you eat her tantalizing chili.

Makes 10 servings

1	16-ounce bag dried pinto beans
2	pounds lean beef sirloin, diced small
1	tablespoon vegetable oil
2	large onions, minced
8	large cloves garlic, chopped
1	green bell pepper, chopped
	vegetable oil spray
1	15-ounce and 2 29-ounce cans Mexican-style (or regular) tomato sauce
3	tablespoons Worcestershire sauce
1	tablespoon chili powder
1	tablespoon cumin
3	tablespoons minced fresh cilantro
1	7-ounce can diced green chilies
1	cup catsup
1	cup water
1	12-ounce can flat beer
	salt to taste

Cover beans and soak in water overnight. Drain beans and cook in salted water for 2 hours. Drain beans again.

Sauté beef in oil. Put beans and beef into a large Dutch oven. Sauté onion, garlic, and bell pepper in a nonstick pan sprayed with vegetable oil spray, until onion is soft. Add vegetables to beans. Add remaining ingredients and blend well. Cook over low heat for 2 hours, stirring often so chili does not stick.

Each serving provides:

395	Calories	54 g	Carbohydrates
32 g	Protein	1,114 mg	Sodium
7 g	Fat	55 mg	Cholesterol
7 g	Dietary Fiber		

Spicy Beef

I've eaten a similar dish for years at a favorite restaurant of mine and finally had to try to make it up at home. This did it. It's delicious. Bottles of Chinese five spices are available in the Oriental section of many supermarkets.

Makes 4 servings

1	pound lean sirloin, sliced 1/8-inch thick
6	cloves garlic, minced
2	tablespoons hoisin sauce
	vegetable oil spray
1	tablespoon oyster sauce
3	tablespoons brown sugar
1	tablespoon catsup
2	tablespoons lite soy sauce
	pinch of Chinese five spices
1/2	teaspoon white pepper
	chili oil to taste (I love this hot)

Slice meat very thin (it helps to freeze meat for about 3 hours and then slice). Rub garlic and hoisin sauce into beef. Marinate 20 minutes. Heat a saucepan and spray with vegetable oil spray. Sauté meat in small batches until barely pink. Add oyster sauce, brown sugar, catsup, soy sauce, Chinese five spices, and white pepper. Cook until sugar has melted and everything is well combined. Add chili oil to taste. Chili oil is very hot so be careful.

You can serve this on rice, rice noodles, or in steamed buns.

Each serving provides:

220	Calories	17 g	Carbohydrates
26 g	Protein	849 mg	Sodium
5 g	Fat	69 mg	Cholesterol
0 g	Dietary Fiber		

Beef in Creamy Mushroom Sauce

This is like a lowfat stroganoff and a good way to take care of a craving for beef without eating too much meat.

Makes 6 servings

1	pound beef sirloin, cut into 1/4-inch strips
5	cloves garlic, minced
1	tablespoon flour mixed with 2 tablespoons water
1	tablespoon butter
1/4	cup sliced green onion
3/4	cup sliced shiitake mushrooms
	vegetable oil spray
1-1/4	cups defatted beef broth
1/2	cup red wine
1	tablespoon tomato paste
1	cup fatfree sour cream
	salt and pepper to taste
8	ounces dry eggless noodles cooked

Mix meat and garlic together. Coat all meat with flour and water mixture. Sauté meat in butter, removing when brown. Do not overcook.

In the same pan, sauté green onion and mushrooms, adding some vegetable oil spray if necessary. Add broth, wine, and tomato paste and cook for 3 minutes. Return meat to pan. Add sour cream and continue cooking slowly (do not let bubble after adding sour cream) until smooth and well blended. Add salt and pepper to taste. If necessary you can thicken sauce with a mixture of cornstarch and water. Serve over cooked noodles.

Each serving provides:

307	Calories	33 g	Carbohydrates
25 g	Protein	295 mg	Sodium
6 g	Fat	51 mg	Cholesterol
2 g	Dietary Fiber		

Pork Tenderloin in Fruit Sauce

I like this combination of sweet and spicy flavors.

Makes 8 servings

Roast:
1-1/2	pounds pork tenderloins
6	cloves garlic, minced
	salt and pepper to taste
	rosemary

Fruit sauce:
1/4	cup chopped dried peaches
1/4	cup chopped dried cranberries
2	cups peach schnapps
1	cup defatted chicken broth
1	cup peach nectar
1/2	onion, minced
1/2	teaspoon dried rosemary
	salt and pepper to taste
1	teaspoon butter sprinkles
1	tablespoon cornstarch mixed with 2 tablespoons water

Preheat oven to 400°.

Rub tenderloins with garlic, salt, pepper, and rosemary. Lay tenderloins on a rack in a roasting pan. Bake for 50 minutes.

To make sauce: Mix dried fruit, peach schnapps, broth, peach nectar, onion, and 1/2 teaspoon rosemary. Cook until liquid has reduced to 2 cups. Season with salt and pepper to taste and add butter sprinkles.

When roast is done, remove it to a warm plate. Add sauce to the roasting pan. Cook a few minutes, scraping up any bits from the bottom of the pan and then thicken with the cornstarch mixture. Slice meat and serve with sauce.

Each serving provides:

243	Calories	31 g	Carbohydrates
18 g	Protein	190 mg	Sodium
5 g	Fat	56 mg	Cholesterol
1 g	Dietary Fiber		

Pork Tenderloin with Apples

The taste of the spicy, garlicky meat with the slightly sweet applesauce is very appealing.

Makes 6 servings

1-1/2 pounds pork tenderloin
      vegetable oil spray
1 teaspoon butter
1 shallot, minced
5 cloves garlic, minced
1-1/2 cups peeled and diced apples
1/2 cup defatted chicken broth
1/4 cup apple cider
3 tablespoons brandy
1-1/2 teaspoons brown sugar
1-1/2 teaspoons fines herbes
      salt and freshly ground pepper to taste
2 teaspoons cornstarch mixed with 2 tablespoons water

Cut pork into 12 slices. Spray a nonstick frying pan with vegetable oil spray. Add pork and cook over high heat until browned. Do not overcook. Remove meat. Add 1 teaspoon butter, shallot, garlic, and apples. Sauté over low heat about 5 minutes. Add broth, cider, brandy, sugar, and fines herbes. Add salt and pepper to taste. Cook, scraping bottom of pan, for 2 more minutes. Thicken with cornstarch and water mixture. Add meat and heat through. Serve 2 slices per person with the applesauce spooned over the meat.

Each serving provides:

211	Calories	8 g	Carbohydrates
24 g	Protein	146 mg	Sodium
7 g	Fat	77 mg	Cholesterol
1 g	Dietary Fiber		

Pork Tenderloin with Garlic and Rosemary

Easy, fast, and a terrific company dish.

Makes 6 servings

2	1-pound pork tenderloins
6	cloves garlic, minced
	salt
	freshly ground black pepper
	fresh rosemary
3	tablespoons flour
2	teaspoons butter
1-1/2	cups defatted chicken broth
2	tablespoons whiskey

Preheat oven to 400°.

Rub pork on all sides with garlic. Sprinkle with salt, pepper, and rosemary. Put on a rack in a roasting pan and bake for 45 to 50 minutes.

Remove rack and meat from pan and set aside. Add flour and butter to roasting pan. Add chicken broth and stir until flour is incorporated. Cook, stirring, until sauce begins to thicken. Add whiskey and salt and pepper to taste, cooking 1 more minute. Slice pork very thin and serve with sauce. The butter can be left out of the recipe by adding the broth, deglazing the pan, and then adding cornstarch instead of flour for thickening. The flavor will not be as rich but it will still be very good.

Each serving provides:

254	Calories	4 g	Carbohydrates
32 g	Protein	334 mg	Sodium
10 g	Fat	103 mg	Cholesterol
0 g	Dietary Fiber		

Pork Leg Roast with Garlicky Gravy

A pork leg makes a wonderful roast and loves lots of garlic on it. An added bonus is the fantastic aroma while it cooks with all that garlic.

Makes 12 servings

Roast:

1	3-pound boneless pork leg roast
8	whole cloves garlic
3	cloves garlic, minced
1	tablespoon chopped fresh thyme
1	tablespoon chopped fresh rosemary
	salt and pepper

Garlicky gravy:

1/2	cup flour
1/2	cup defatted chicken broth
1/2	cup defatted beef broth
1/2	cup nonfat milk
1	teaspoon black pepper
1	teaspoon salt
1	teaspoon dried thyme
1/4	cup brandy
2	teaspoons browning and seasoning sauce (such as Kitchen Bouquet®) (optional)

Preheat oven to 400°.

Cut 8 slits in your roast and push a garlic clove into each slit. Rub the minced garlic all over the outside of the roast. Sprinkle the roast with the fresh thyme and rosemary, salt, and pepper. Place on a rack on a roasting pan. Bake roast in a 400° oven for 15 minutes. Turn oven down to 350° and cook for 2 more hours. Remove meat from pan and drain all fat out of pan.

To make gravy: With roasting pan off heat, add flour and stir around pan, scraping brown bits as you do. Do this until flour is no longer white. Warm chicken broth, beef broth, and milk in microwave and then stir into flour mixture, whisking as you do. Return pan to heat and cook, blending flour and liquid, until gravy

continued on next page

begins to thicken. Stir in 1 teaspoon pepper, 1 teaspoon salt, 1 teaspoon thyme, and brandy. Continue cooking until smooth. Taste and adjust seasoning if necessary. Add browning and seasoning sauce if you want a darker gravy.

Each serving provides:			
320	Calories	6 g	Carbohydrates
21 g	Protein	318 mg	Sodium
22 g	Fat	83 mg	Cholesterol
0 g	Dietary Fiber		

Pork Rolls with Apricot Sauce

Makes 6 servings

Pork rolls:

1	6-1/4-ounce package wild and brown rice mix
4	cloves garlic, minced
2	tablespoons minced dried tomatoes
1/4	cup minced mushrooms
1	tablespoon minced celery
2	egg whites
12	1/2-inch slices lean pork (about 1-1/2 pounds)
1/2	cup flour
	vegetable oil spray

Apricot sauce:

1	cup apricot nectar
1	tablespoon lite soy sauce
1/2	cup marsala
1	cup defatted chicken broth
2	cloves garlic, minced
1	teaspoon *each* pepper and sugar
1	teaspoon dried chervil
2	teaspoons cornstarch mixed with 1 tablespoon water (optional)

Mix rice mix, 4 cloves minced garlic, tomatoes, mushrooms, and celery and cook as directed on package (eliminating butter or oil). When rice is done and cool, stir in egg whites.

Lay out pork slices. Spread some rice mixture on each pork slice. Roll up and tie with kitchen twine. Dredge each roll in flour. Sauté in a nonstick pan sprayed with vegetable oil spray until browned. When finished, remove rolls from pan.

To make sauce: Add apricot nectar, soy sauce, marsala, broth, 2 cloves minced garlic, pepper, sugar, and chervil to pan. Blend well and return pork rolls to pan. Cover, and simmer for 20 minutes. Remove cover and add cornstarch mixture if sauce needs thickening. Cook 10 more minutes.

Each serving provides:

387	Calories	43 g	Carbohydrates
31 g	Protein	870 mg	Sodium
7 g	Fat	67 mg	Cholesterol
1 g	Dietary Fiber		

Lasagna al Mare with
Creamy Tomato Sauce

Molly's Sauce for Macaroni

Mushroom Pasta

Pasta Shells Florentine with White Sauce

Chicken and Broccoli Pasta

Chicken Pasta with Plum Wine

Light Paella

Rice-Stuffed Tomatoes

Savory Rice

Mashed-Potato Bake

Spicy Potato Bake

Crispy Potato Bake

Wonderful Garlic Mashed Potatoes

Sweet and Spicy Sweet Potatoes

Sweet Potato Bake

Baked Beans

Three Bean Mix on Crispy Polenta

8

Pasta, Rice, Potatoes, and Beans

Y ou can make thousands of dishes using these nutritious (and lowfat) complex carbohydrates. And all of these foods thrive with the addition of lots of garlic.

Pasta, which is ever so popular today (we can attest to this by the amount of pasta restaurants popping up on every corner), is an excellent food. It has come a long way in the last few years and you can now find nearly every color and flavor imaginable in the grocery store. Pasta is easy to make from scratch, fast and easy to cook, and delightful combined with meats, fish, poultry, and vegetables to make a warm, filling, and healthful main dish.

Rice also blends well with many ingredients. It is the principal food for many countries and has now risen in popularity in the United States. Try blending your favorite ingredients into a rice dish using garlic as a dominant ingredient.

America loves potatoes! The potato should become a major part of any lowfat diet. Many people can make a meal out of a potato. The lowfat potato recipes included here are as tasty (or tastier) than their heavy, fat-laden counterparts.

I keep my kitchen well-stocked with a variety of dried beans. Beans are a wonderful source of protein, are high in fiber, and are rich in vitamin B. Best of all, beans are truly versatile and their warm, robust flavor is well complemented by garlic.

Lasagna al Mare with Creamy Tomato Sauce

I have made things quick and easy in this recipe by using egg-roll wraps for the lasagna noodles. You can use the thicker dried lasagna noodle or make homemade lasagna noodles if you prefer.

Makes 12 servings

Lasagna:

1	tablespoon olive oil
1	pound shrimp, shelled, deveined, and coarsely chopped
6	cloves garlic, minced
1/4	cup chopped green onion
1/2	pound mushrooms, thinly sliced
1	teaspoon salt
1/2	teaspoon pepper
1	cup fatfree ricotta cheese
12	ounces cooked crabmeat
1	egg white
1	12-ounce package egg-roll wraps

Sauce:

8	ounces clam juice
2	cups Italian-style tomato sauce
1	cup lite evaporated milk
1/2	cup vermouth
1	teaspoon salt
1/2	teaspoon white pepper
1/2	teaspoon butter sprinkles
1/4	cup Parmesan cheese (save 1 tablespoon for topping)
2	tablespoons cornstarch mixed with 3 tablespoons wine fresh Italian parsley, chopped, for garnish

Preheat oven to 350°.

To prepare the filling: Heat the olive oil and sauté the shrimp and garlic until shrimp begins to turn pink. Add the green onion, mushrooms, salt, and pepper and cook 1 more minute. Transfer the mixture to a bowl. Add the ricotta, crabmeat, and egg white. Mix well and set aside.

continued on next page

To make the sauce: Put clam juice, tomato sauce, evaporated milk, vermouth, salt, pepper, and butter sprinkles into a saucepan. Cook slowly for 2 minutes, until everything has blended. Add the Parmesan cheese and cook 2 more minutes. Stir in cornstarch mixture and cook until sauce thickens. Remove from heat.

To assemble lasagna: Spread 3/4 cup of the sauce on the bottom of a 9 × 13-inch baking dish. Dip egg-roll wraps in hot water and shake off excess water. Lay 6 egg-roll wrap on the sauce to cover the bottom of the dish. Layer with the filling and some more sauce. Starting with the egg-roll wraps, layer again, finishing with another layer of egg-roll wraps. Spread the remaining sauce over the last layer of noodles and sprinkle with the reserved 1 tablespoon Parmesan cheese.

Bake for 30 to 40 minutes or until bubbly and lightly browned. Sprinkle with chopped Italian parsley.

Each serving provides:

239	Calories	27 g	Carbohydrates
21 g	Protein	960 mg	Sodium
4 g	Fat	82 mg	Cholesterol
0 g	Dietary Fiber		

Molly's Sauce for Macaroni

Molly was my husband's grandmother. She has been gone for many years and we dearly miss her. I loved to go visit her and Pa Dutch (grandpa Ferrari). She was a wonderful cook and she made this favorite sauce all the time. I have only changed the recipe to remove the ful content.

Makes 6 servings

1	2 × 2-inch piece of lean beef (1/2 pound)
1	tablespoon olive oil
1	yellow onion, thinly sliced
6	cloves garlic, minced
1/2	cup chopped parsley (Molly's recipe said one handful)
1	cup dried mushrooms, covered with hot water and soaked
1	29-ounce can tomato sauce
1	teaspoon sugar
	salt and pepper to taste
12	ounces dry pasta, cooked

Use a nonstick saucepan. Sauté beef in olive oil until beef has browned on both sides. Add onion, garlic, and parsley to meat and continue to cook until onions are soft. After soaking, add dried mushrooms to sauce. Reserve the mushroom water and let it sit to settle the sediment. Add tomato sauce and sugar to the sauce. When the mushroom water has settled add it, not the substance on the bottom, to the sauce. Add 6 more cups water to the sauce. Mix well. Let sauce cook slowly for at least 2 hours.

When the sauce has finished cooking, put the mushrooms and meat in a food processor and shred with the metal blade. Return shredded mushrooms and meat to the sauce and continue to simmer, while cooking pasta until pasta is done. Serve sauce over pasta.

Each serving provides:

354	Calories	60 g	Carbohydrates
19 g	Protein	858 mg	Sodium
5 g	Fat	22 mg	Cholesterol
4 g	Dietary Fiber		

Mushroom Pasta

My daughters Suzy and Carrie went to Italy with me recently. Some friends served us this pasta dish the first night we arrived. It was so wonderful that my girls have been asking me to make a similar recipe ever since. Well, here it is. It not only tastes like our Italian friends' pasta, but I have cut out almost all of the fat. This is definitely a mushroom lover's fantasy.

Makes 6 servings

1	tablespoon virgin olive oil
5	cloves garlic, minced
2	leeks, white part only, thinly sliced
1	pound mushrooms, sliced
1/2	teaspoon vegetable seasoning (such as Vegit®)
2	tablespoons chopped parsley
1/4	teaspoon dried oregano
1	cup lite evaporated milk
1	cup fatfree sour cream
1/2	cup defatted chicken broth
1/2	cup white wine
1	tablespoon cornstarch mixed with 3 tablespoons wine
1	teaspoon butter sprinkles
1/3	cup freshly grated Parmesan cheese
	salt and freshly ground pepper to taste
9	ounces dry tube pasta

Sauté the garlic and leeks in the virgin olive oil until leeks become soft. Add the mushrooms and vegetable seasoning and cook slowly until liquid from mushrooms evaporates. You want the mushrooms to brown slightly, not burn. Add the parsley, oregano, evaporated milk, sour cream, broth, and wine to the pan and cook 2 minutes. Stir in the cornstarch mixture and simmer until mixture thickens. Stir in butter sprinkles and Parmesan cheese. Season with salt and freshly ground pepper. Cook 1 more minute.

Cook pasta according to package directions. Drain and toss pasta with sauce. Can be served immediately or put into a 325° oven, covered, for 15 minutes.

Mushroom Lasagna

To make this into lasagna, prepare the sauce as above. Then, because this is a delicate sauce, I like to use egg-roll wraps or home-made noodles (see Basics) for the lasagna. If you are using noodles, and not egg-roll wraps, precook the noodles. Egg-roll wraps just need to be dipped in hot water before layering. Put a little sauce in the bottom of a 9 × 13-inch baking pan and make alternating layers of the noodles and sauce, ending with the sauce. Cover, and bake in a 375° oven for 20 minutes.

Each serving provides:

333	Calories	49 g	Carbohydrates
16 g	Protein	312 mg	Sodium
6 g	Fat	11 mg	Cholesterol
2 g	Dietary Fiber		

Pasta Shells Florentine with White Sauce

I like to make lots of stuffed shells at once and freeze several pans. This makes for easy future meals. The shells freeze very well. If you freeze them, thaw before cooking and cook as directed, or partially thaw and increase cooking time by 20 minutes.

Makes 10 servings

Stuffed shells:

20	jumbo pasta shells
1/2	cup minced celery
1/2	onion, minced
5	cloves garlic, minced
1	tablespoon virgin olive oil
2	cups nonfat cottage cheese
1	10-ounce package frozen chopped spinach, cooked and drained
1/2	cup dried tomatoes, soaked and slivered
1	egg white
1/2	teaspoon salt
1/2	teaspoon pepper
1/2	teaspoon dried oregano
1/2	teaspoon dried basil
	pinch of nutmeg

White sauce:

2	tablespoons minced onion
3	cloves garlic, minced
	olive oil spray
2	cups nonfat milk
1	cup defatted chicken broth
1	teaspoon butter sprinkles
1	tablespoon cornstarch mixed with 1/3 cup white wine
1/3	cup freshly grated Parmesan cheese
	salt and freshly ground pepper to taste

Preheat oven to 375°.

Cook pasta shells according to package directions. Drain and let sit in cold water.

Sauté celery, onion, and garlic in oil until onion is tender. Combine sautéed vegetables with cottage cheese, spinach, dried tomato,

egg white, salt, pepper, oregano, basil, and nutmeg. Mix well. Fill
shells with cottage cheese-spinach mixture.

To prepare sauce: Sauté onion and garlic in olive oil spray until
onion is soft. Add milk, broth, butter sprinkles, and cornstarch-
wine mixture. Cook until sauce thickens. Stir in Parmesan cheese.

Pour half the sauce into a 12-inch square baking pan. Arrange
stuffed shells in baking pan on top of sauce. Cover with remaining
sauce. Bake, covered, for 25 minutes. Uncover and bake 10 more
minutes.

Each serving provides:

199	Calories	29 g	Carbohydrates
14 g	Protein	511 mg	Sodium
3 g	Fat	8 mg	Cholesterol
2 g	Dietary Fiber		

Chicken and Broccoli Pasta

I like to freshly grate dry cheese onto each serving of pasta instead of using pre-grated cheese. The flavor is stronger and so much better, especially when we use so little. You'll love this quick and easy dish.

Makes 6 servings

2	teaspoons cornstarch mixed with 2 tablespoons water
6	cloves garlic, chopped
2	tablespoons sliced green onion
4	chicken breasts, boned, skinned, and diced
1	tablespoon butter
2	cups broccoli (cut into small flowerets)
1/2	cup slivered dried tomatoes
1-1/2	cups defatted chicken broth
1/2	cup white wine
1-1/2	tablespoons cornstarch mixed with 3 tablespoons water
9	ounces spiral-shaped pasta, cooked
	Asiago cheese to freshly grate over pasta

Mix 2 teaspoons cornstarch mixture, garlic, and green onion with the diced chicken. Sauté the chicken in a teaspoon of butter at a time, doing only 1/4 of the chicken at one time. Do this on high heat so chicken browns but does not get too done. Remove chicken and set aside. To the same pan, add the broccoli, tomatoes, broth, and wine and cook until broccoli is tender. Add the browned chicken and 1-1/2 tablespoons cornstarch mixture and cook all until broth has thickened. Cover, and cook 2 more minutes. Mix in cooked pasta and serve with a little freshly grated cheese.

Each serving provides:

414	Calories	42 g	Carbohydrates
45 g	Protein	390 mg	Sodium
5 g	Fat	96 mg	Cholesterol
3 g	Dietary Fiber		

Chicken Pasta with Plum Wine

A splendid blend of flavors that makes a very special first course.

Makes 4 main-dish or 6 first-course servings

2	whole chicken breasts, boned, and skinned
	slice of onion
	stalk of celery
	butter-flavored vegetable oil spray
2	tablespoons chopped green onion
5	cloves garlic, minced
2	tablespoons minced celery
1/3	cup shredded carrot
1/3	cup finely diced red bell pepper
1	tablespoon minced parsley
3	tablespoons pinenuts
1/4	cup fatfree sour cream
3/4	cup lite evaporated milk
1	teaspoon dried thyme
1/2	cup plum wine
3	teaspoons cornstarch mixed with 2 tablespoons of the wine
9	ounces dry pasta, cooked
	salt and freshly ground pepper to taste
	Asiago cheese to freshly grate over pasta

Poach the chicken breasts in water with a slice of onion and a stalk of celery until tender. Dice the chicken and set aside.

In a nonstick pan sprayed with butter-flavored vegetable oil spray, sauté the green onion, garlic, minced celery, carrot, bell pepper, and parsley until vegetables just begin to soften. Add pinenuts, sour cream, evaporated milk, thyme, and wine. Mix well. Add chicken to the pan and cook 5 minutes. Mix in cornstarch and wine mixture, and cook until sauce thickens. Cook pasta in salted water until done. Drain and mix with hot chicken sauce. Season with salt and freshly ground pepper and a small sprinkling of cheese.

Each main-dish serving provides:

533	Calories	64 g	Carbohydrates
42 g	Protein	152 mg	Sodium
7 g	Fat	76 mg	Cholesterol
2 g	Dietary Fiber		

Light Paella

Paella makes a lovely and satisfying meal. I have omitted the sausage to lighten the dish.

Makes 8 servings

	vegetable oil spray
1	small green bell pepper, diced
1	small red bell pepper, diced
1	onion, minced
6	cloves garlic, thinly sliced
1-1/4 to 1-3/4 cups defatted chicken broth
1/4	cup white wine
1-1/4 cups water
2	large tomatoes, peeled and chopped
1	teaspoon salt
1	teaspoon freshly ground pepper
1/4	teaspoon ground saffron
1-1/4 cups raw rice
2/3	cup peas
2/3	cup artichoke hearts
3	half chicken breasts, browned and cut into 4 pieces each
1/2	pound shrimp, peeled and cleaned
	hot steamed crab legs or crawfish for garnish (optional)

Preheat oven to 350°.

Spray a nonstick pan with vegetable oil spray and sauté bell peppers, onion, and garlic over low heat for about 5 minutes until onion begins to soften. Stir in 1-1/4 cups broth (reserve 1/2 cup), wine, water, tomatoes, salt, and pepper. Bring to a boil and then add remaining ingredients. Blend well and return to boiling. Cover, and bake 45 minutes or until rice is tender. Check liquid while baking; if too dry you can add additional 1/4 to 1/2 cup broth. Fluff when done and serve on a heated plate. I like to garnish this dish with some hot steamed crab legs or crawfish.

Each serving provides:			
257	Calories	32 g	Carbohydrates
18 g	Protein	536 mg	Sodium
5 g	Fat	64 mg	Cholesterol
2 g	Dietary Fiber		

Rice-Stuffed Tomatoes

A side dish with a unique flavor. Coconut milk lends a wonderful taste to Thai and Chinese cooking as well as this recipe. You can find it in supermarkets and Oriental grocery stores.

Makes 10 servings

10	medium-small tomatoes
1	teaspoon butter
2	tablespoons thinly sliced green onion
1/2	cup shredded carrot
4	cloves garlic, minced
2/3	cup lowfat coconut milk (such as A Taste of Thai brand)
2-3/4	cups water
2	cups uncooked long-grain rice
1/2	teaspoon cumin
1	cup small peas
1/4	cup sliced almonds

Peel and cut off top third of tomatoes. Spoon out inside of tomatoes and put aside.

Sauté the green onion, carrot, and garlic in the butter in a nonstick saucepan for 3 minutes. Add coconut milk, water, rice, cumin, peas, and almonds. Mix well. Cover, and cook over low heat for 25 minutes or until liquid has evaporated. Dip the tomatoes in boiling water or microwave a few minutes before filling with rice, so the tomatoes do not cool rice. Fluff rice and spoon into tomatoes.

Each serving provides:

223	Calories	39 g	Carbohydrates
5 g	Protein	21 mg	Sodium
6 g	Fat	1 mg	Cholesterol
2 g	Dietary Fiber		

Savory Rice

Makes 8 servings

1/2   cup chopped mushrooms
1/4   cup minced green onion
1/2   cup minced yellow bell pepper
4   cloves garlic, chopped
3-1/2 cups defatted chicken broth
1   teaspoon dried summer savory
1   teaspoon vegetable seasoning (such as Vegit®)
1   tablespoon minced fresh parsley
1   tomato, peeled, seeded, and chopped
1-1/2 cups uncooked rice
        salt and pepper to taste

Put mushrooms, green onion, bell pepper, and garlic into a saucepan with 1/2 cup of the chicken broth and cook, stirring, until vegetables begin to soften. Add remaining ingredients, bring to a boil, and cook until liquid has absorbed. This takes about 20 to 25 minutes. Fluff rice and serve.

Each serving provides:

149	Calories	31 g	Carbohydrates
4 g	Protein	461 mg	Sodium
1 g	Fat	0 mg	Cholesterol
1 g	Dietary Fiber		

Mashed-Potato Bake

If you are lucky enough to have any of these potatoes left over, make a patty and fry it in a nonstick pan sprayed with vegetable oil spray for a delicious breakfast treat.

Makes 8 servings

10	medium potatoes, peeled and quartered
4	ounces fatfree cream cheese
2	egg whites
1/4	cup chopped green onion
4	cloves garlic, minced
2	tablespoons chopped fresh parsley
	vegetable seasoning (such as Vegit®)
	freshly ground pepper
	vegetable oil spray
1	teaspoon butter (optional)

Preheat oven to 350°.

Put potatoes in a pan and cover with water. Bring to a boil and cook for about 15 minutes or until fork-tender. Drain and mash. Add cream cheese and mix well. Stir in egg whites, green onion, garlic, and parsley. Season to taste with vegetable seasoning and freshly ground pepper. Blend thoroughly. Put into a baking dish sprayed with vegetable oil spray. Dot with butter if desired. Bake for 30 minutes.

Each serving provides:

150	Calories	31 g	Carbohydrates
7 g	Protein	124 mg	Sodium
0 g	Fat	3 mg	Cholesterol
3 g	Dietary Fiber		

Spicy Potato Bake

These potatoes are just as delicious for breakfast as they are for dinner.

Makes 8 servings

	olive oil spray
2-1/2	pounds little red potatoes, parboiled and halved
1	bunch green onions, diced
6	large cloves garlic, chopped
1	green bell pepper, diced small
2	tablespoons minced parsley
2	tablespoons minced fresh basil
2	teaspoons cracked black pepper
1	teaspoon dried oregano
	vegetable seasoning (such as Vegit®) to taste
1/2	cup grated fatfree sharp cheddar cheese
1	cup nonfat cottage cheese and 1/2 cup fatfree sour cream blended together

Preheat oven to 375°.

Spray a nonstick skillet with olive oil spray. Add potatoes, green onions, and garlic. Sauté until potatoes start to brown. Add the next 6 ingredients and cook 2 more minutes. Mix grated cheese into the sour cream-cottage cheese mixture and stir into potatoes. Spoon all into a baking pan that has been sprayed with olive oil spray. Bake for 30 to 40 minutes or until potatoes are nice and browned.

Each serving provides:

174	Calories	32 g	Carbohydrates
10 g	Protein	198 mg	Sodium
1 g	Fat	3 mg	Cholesterol
3 g	Dietary Fiber		

Crispy Potato Bake

Makes 6 servings

4	large baking potatoes
	salt
1	teaspoon butter
2	shallots, chopped
4	cloves garlic, chopped
1/2	cup nonfat milk
1	cup defatted chicken broth
2	teaspoons cornstarch mixed with 2 tablespoons of the broth
	butter-flavored vegetable oil spray
	vegetable seasoning (such as Vegit®) to taste
	freshly ground pepper to taste
1/2	cup bread crumbs
2	tablespoons grated Parmesan cheese

Preheat oven to 375°.

Peel and gently boil whole potatoes in salted water for 30 minutes or until tender. Cool potatoes and thinly slice. Set aside.

Sauté the shallots and garlic in the butter for 2 to 3 minutes. Add the milk and broth and blend. Cook until mixture is hot. Stir in cornstarch mixture and cook until sauce begins to thicken just a little.

Spray a baking pan with butter-flavored vegetable oil spray. Spread a layer of potatoes in the pan and sprinkle with vegetable seasoning and pepper. Pour a little sauce over the potatoes and continue to layer this way, ending with sauce. Mix the bread crumbs and Parmesan cheese together and sprinkle over all. Spray with some butter-flavored vegetable oil spray. Bake for 30 minutes or until nicely browned.

Each serving provides:

161	Calories	30 g	Carbohydrates
6 g	Protein	298 mg	Sodium
2 g	Fat	3 mg	Cholesterol
2 g	Dietary Fiber		

Wonderful Garlic Mashed Potatoes

Makes 6 to 8 servings

3	pounds russet potatoes
1/3	cup nonfat milk
1/4	cup lite evaporated milk
2	tablespoons fatfree cream cheese
1	head garlic, roasted (see Basics)
	salt and pepper to taste
	vegetable oil spray
2	teaspoons melted butter (optional)

Peel and boil potatoes until tender. Drain and mash potatoes. Add nonfat milk, evaporated milk, cream cheese, and squeezed garlic. Season with salt and pepper. Spoon into an ovenproof casserole sprayed with vegetable oil spray and drizzle with butter if you like. You can let this warm in a 250° oven for 20 minutes or serve immediately.

Each serving provides:

174	Calories	37 g	Carbohydrates
6 g	Protein	81 mg	Sodium
1 g	Fat	2 mg	Cholesterol
3 g	Dietary Fiber		

Sweet and Spicy Sweet Potatoes

The roasted garlic gives a pleasant nutty taste to this recipe.

Makes 8 servings

3	large sweet potatoes
1	teaspoon butter
1	head garlic, roasted (see Basics)
1	teaspoon dried thyme
1	lemon, washed and thinly sliced
	juice of 2 lemons
1/3	cup brown sugar
1/2	teaspoon nutmeg
3	tablespoons maple syrup
1/4	cup sherry

Gently boil sweet potatoes until tender. Let cool slightly and peel. Slice sweet potatoes about 1/4-inch thick. Put butter, garlic, thyme, lemon slices, lemon juice, sugar, nutmeg, and maple syrup into a nonstick pan. Stir in sherry and warm until sugar dissolves. Add sweet potatoes. Cook carefully, gently lifting sweet potatoes to mix well until sauce thickens and covers potatoes nicely.

Each serving provides:

170	Calories	39 g	Carbohydrates
2 g	Protein	41 mg	Sodium
1 g	Fat	1 mg	Cholesterol
2 g	Dietary Fiber		

Sweet Potato Bake

A great side dish at Thanksgiving—you can assemble this ahead of time and refrigerate it until you're ready to bake it.

Makes 8 servings

4	cups cooked and mashed sweet potatoes
1/2	cup fatfree cream cheese
6	cloves garlic, slivered and roasted (see Basics)
3	tablespoons maple syrup
1/2	cup lite evaporated milk
2	egg whites
	vegetable oil spray
1/3	cup rolled oats
1/3	cup brown sugar
1/4	cup cake flour
1	tablespoon lemon rind
	juice of 1 lemon
1	tablespoon unsalted butter, melted

Preheat oven to 325°.

Mix sweet potatoes, cream cheese, garlic, maple syrup, and evaporated milk together. Mix in egg whites. Spoon into a baking dish sprayed with vegetable oil spray.

Mix the oats, sugar, flour, lemon rind, lemon juice, and melted butter together and sprinkle over the sweet potatoes. Bake, uncovered, for 50 minutes.

Each serving provides:

302	Calories	62 g	Carbohydrates
9 g	Protein	156 mg	Sodium
3 g	Fat	9 mg	Cholesterol
5 g	Dietary Fiber		

Baked Beans

I find that the smoke flavoring gives the same taste as ham to this lowfat version of an American favorite.

Makes 6 servings

	vegetable oil spray
2	cups dried navy beans, cooked (see Basics) and liquid reserved
1	onion, chopped
6	cloves garlic, chopped
1	cup tomato juice
1/4	cup dark molasses
1-1/2	teaspoons smoke flavoring, or to taste
1	teaspoon salt
2	teaspoons Dijon mustard
1	teaspoon Worcestershire sauce
1	tablespoon brown sugar

Preheat oven to 300°.

Spray the inside of a casserole with vegetable oil spray. Pour cooked beans and their liquid into casserole. Mix remaining ingredients together with the beans. Cover and bake for 4 to 5 hours.

Each serving provides:

299	Calories	58 g	Carbohydrates
16 g	Protein	592 mg	Sodium
1 g	Fat	0 mg	Cholesterol
7 g	Dietary Fiber		

Three Bean Mix on Crispy Polenta

The spicy beans are delicious served on the Crispy Polenta. They're also good spooned into a pita or wrapped in a flour tortilla.

Makes 12 servings

Three bean mix:

	olive oil spray
1	whole chicken breast, boned, skinned, and diced small
1/3	cup minced onion
6	cloves garlic, minced
1/2	cup diced green bell pepper
1/2	cup diced red bell pepper
1	8-ounce can garbanzo beans, drained
1	8-ounce can kidney beans, drained
1	8-ounce can lima beans, drained
1/2	teaspoon ground cloves
1/2	teaspoon dried ginger
1	tablespoon Worcestershire sauce
4	drops chili oil
1/3	cup brown sugar
2	tablespoons apple cider vinegar
1	cup crushed pineapple
1	tablespoon chopped fresh cilantro

Polenta:

4	cups water
1	teaspoon salt
1	cup yellow polenta
2	cloves garlic, minced
	olive oil spray

Spray a nonstick pan with olive oil spray and sauté chicken, onion, and garlic for 3 minutes. Add bell peppers and cook, stirring, for 3 more minutes. Add beans, cloves, ginger, Worcestershire sauce, chili oil, brown sugar, vinegar, and pineapple. Simmer for about 5 minutes or until chicken is cooked through. Stir in cilantro and cook 2 more minutes.

To make polenta: Combine water, salt, polenta, and garlic and stir well. Bring to a boil and continue stirring. Watch carefully and stir often until polenta pulls away from the sides of the pan. This will take about 15 minutes. Transfer the polenta to a jelly roll pan and spread out thinly. Cover pan with plastic wrap and refrigerate (this can be made the day before). When chilled, cut polenta into 3-inch squares. Sauté in a nonstick pan sprayed with olive oil spray until crisp on both sides. Serve each polenta square with 1/2 cup of the Three Bean Mix.

Each serving provides:			
150	Calories	27 g	Carbohydrates
8 g	Protein	305 mg	Sodium
1 g	Fat	11 mg	Cholesterol
3 g	Dietary Fiber		

Dark Savory Prune Bread

Herbed Cottage Cheese Bread

Peppered Wheat Bread

Garlic Sticks

Focaccia

Pizza Dough

Vegetable Pizza

Garlicky Lettuce and Tomato Pizza

Spicy Corn Bread

Garlic and Dill Muffins

Garlic and Sour Cream Biscuits

9

Breads, Pizzas, Muffins, and Biscuits

Baking fresh bread is one of my favorite things to do. I enjoy the entire sensual process of mixing, kneading, punching, and, finally, smelling the cozy aroma while it bakes.

I always tell my students not to be afraid of making bread. You may not be successful the first few times, but please don't give up. It takes everyone a few times to really get the right feel of the dough. Soon you will be able to tell how smooth the dough should be, and recognize the spongy-blistery feeling of the dough after it rises. Then you'll be rewarded with a gratifying feeling of accomplishment and those beautiful, crusty, homemade loaves.

Pizza has a special place in our hearts, and it has never been so good for you as in these recipes. The roasted garlic is so delicious spread on the dough that you won't need all that cheese to enjoy pizza anymore.

Savory fresh-baked muffins are delightful when flavored with garlic and spices and take no time at all to make. Biscuits made from scratch are a little more time-consuming, but so tender and flavorful.

Dark Savory Prune Bread

If you don't have a food processor, the dough can be made in a mixer with a dough hook or the old bowl and wooden spoon way. This is a delightful, full-flavored bread that is delicious with any meal. You can make loaves or rolls, and it makes great toast.

Makes 12 servings

1	cup dried pitted prunes
1	package plus 1 teaspoon dry yeast
1	cup warm water (about 110°)
1-1/2	teaspoons salt
3	cloves garlic, minced
1	teaspoon dried rosemary
4 to 4-1/2 cups flour	
	vegetable oil spray
1	teaspoon melted butter

Preheat oven to 375°.

Put prunes into a saucepan and just cover with water. Cook until prunes are soft and can be pureed. Puree prunes and let cool.

Put yeast in a food processor and add 1/4 cup of the warm water. Pulse a few times and let sit until yeast begins to bubble, about 3 minutes. Add puree of prunes, salt, garlic, rosemary, 2 cups flour, and remaining warm water. Mix well. Add 1-1/2 cups more flour and mix again. Add as much of the remaining cup of flour as is necessary to make a smooth, soft dough.

Spray a bowl with vegetable oil spray and put dough in bowl. Cover with a cloth and let dough rise in a warm place until it has doubled in size. Punch dough down and form into rolls or 2 small loaves. Let rise until doubled in size again. Put dough into 2 loaf pans or muffin tins sprayed with vegetable oil spray. Before putting in oven, brush loaves with melted butter. Bake for about 35 to 40 minutes for 2 small loaves, or until bread has browned on top and bottom.

Each serving provides:

201	Calories	43 g	Carbohydrates
5 g	Protein	280 mg	Sodium
1 g	Fat	1 mg	Cholesterol
2 g	Dietary Fiber		

Herbed Cottage Cheese Bread

This bread makes wonderful rolls, loaves, or braids. Shape it as you like.
Slightly warm the cottage cheese in the microwave (1 minute on low)
before using so that it doesn't slow down the action of the yeast.

Makes 12 servings

1	package plus 1 teaspoon dry yeast
1-1/4	cups warm water (about 110°)
1	tablespoon sugar
2	teaspoons salt
1	teaspoon celery seed
1	teaspoon dill seed
1	tablespoon minced garlic
1	cup nonfat cottage cheese
4 to 4-1/2 cups flour	
	vegetable oil spray

Preheat oven to 400°.

Put yeast, 1/4 cup warm water, and sugar into a food processor
or mixing bowl. Blend and let sit until yeast begins to bubble, about
3 minutes. Add salt, celery seed, dill seed, garlic, cottage cheese,
and 3 cups flour. Add remaining 1 cup warm water and blend. Add
as much of the remaining flour as necessary to make a soft, smooth
dough.

Put dough into a bowl that has been sprayed with vegetable oil
spray and cover with a cloth. Let dough rise until doubled in size,
about 50 minutes. Punch down and shape. Cover dough and let rise
again until doubled in size. Put dough into 2 loaf pans sprayed
with vegetable oil spray.

Bake for 20 to 35 minutes, (depending how you shaped dough),
or until bread is golden brown.

Each serving provides:

187	Calories	37 g	Carbohydrates
7 g	Protein	435 mg	Sodium
1 g	Fat	2 mg	Cholesterol
1 g	Dietary Fiber		

Peppered Wheat Bread

I like to combine whole wheat and unbleached white flour when I make whole wheat bread so that the bread has a lighter texture. The cracked black pepper gives a stronger "bite" than regular ground pepper. I use a pizza brick in my oven to bake this bread on. It makes a nice, crusty loaf.

Makes 12 servings

1	package plus 1 teaspoon dry yeast
1/4	plus 1-1/3 cups warm water (110°)
3	cups unbleached flour
1	cup whole wheat flour
4	cloves garlic, minced
2	teaspoons salt
2	teaspoons cracked black pepper
1/4	cup nonfat cottage cheese
	vegetable oil spray
	spray bottle of water
1	egg white mixed with 1 tablespoon water

Preheat oven to 400°.

Mix the yeast and 1/4 cup warm water with the steel blade of a food processor. Let sit until yeast bubbles, about 3 minutes. Add 2-1/2 cups unbleached flour, 1 cup whole wheat flour, garlic, salt, pepper, and cottage cheese. Pulse a few times. Pour the remaining 1-1/3 cups warm water through the feed tube while the processor is running. Process until smooth. Add a little more flour (a tablespoon at a time), if necessary, to make a smooth dough.

Put dough into a bowl sprayed with vegetable oil spray, cover, and let rise 1 hour in a warm place. Punch dough down and let rise 1 hour more. Remove dough and shape into a log or braid. Put bread on a cookie pan that has been sprayed with vegetable oil spray, cover, and let rise 40 minutes more, or until doubled in size. Bake for 10 minutes. Open oven and spray bread with water, continuing to spray with water every 10 minutes until bread is done. Bread is done when nicely browned and takes about 20 to 30 minutes to bake, depending on how you shaped it.

Each serving provides:

159	Calories	32 g	Carbohydrates
6 g	Protein	390 mg	Sodium
1 g	Fat	0 mg	Cholesterol
2 g	Dietary Fiber		

Garlic Sticks

These wonderful sticks are addictive! I like to make big basketsful for large parties.

Makes 40 sticks
(1 garlic stick per serving)

2	packages dry yeast
1	tablespoon sugar
1-1/3	cups warm water (110°)
1	teaspoon salt
2	teaspoons pepper
8	cloves garlic, minced
2	tablespoons virgin olive oil
3-1/2	cups flour
	vegetable oil spray
1	egg white beaten with 1 tablespoon water
	coarse salt, poppy seeds, sesame seeds, garlic salt, *or* Parmesan cheese for topping

Preheat oven to 375°.

Put yeast, sugar, and 1/3 cup of the warm water into a food processor or heavy mixer. Pulse a few times and let sit a couple of minutes until the yeast starts to bubble. Add salt, pepper, garlic, oil, and 1 cup flour. Blend. Add remaining 1 cup warm water and 2 cups more flour and blend well. Add remaining flour a tablespoon at a time until dough is smooth and pulls away from the sides of the bowl. Remove from processor and knead a few minutes.

Cut dough into 40 equal pieces. (This will make very thin bread-sticks. If you want them thicker cut into 16 or 20 equal pieces.) Roll out each piece of dough into 12- to 14-inch sticks. Put sticks on cookie sheets sprayed with vegetable oil spray, leaving 1/4 inch between each stick. (You can now freeze these in the pans. After the sticks are frozen solid, remove, wrap in bunches in foil, and freeze. Remove when ready to use, and let rise in pans for 45 minutes before baking.) If you are baking the sticks immediately, let sticks rise about 15 minutes. Brush with egg white mixture and sprinkle with desired topping. Bake until browned (about 10 to 12 minutes for thin sticks, 12 to 15 minutes for thick).

Each serving provides:

50	Calories	9 g	Carbohydrates
1 g	Protein	57 mg	Sodium
1 g	Fat	0 mg	Cholesterol
0 g	Dietary Fiber		

Focaccia

I love this versatile flat bread, which is terrific with fresh herbs. Focaccia is normally made plain and then the herbs, tomato sauce, or other ingredients are sprinkled on top of the bread. In this recipe some of the herbs are mixed into the bread. Cottage cheese is added to replace some of the oil that usually adds moistness to the bread. What oil is used should be virgin olive oil, because of its strong, fruity flavor. My favorite way to eat this bread is steaming hot, right out of the oven. It also makes delicious sandwiches.

Makes 12 servings

2	packages dry yeast
1-3/4	cup warm water (110°)
2	teaspoons sugar
1/2	cup nonfat cottage cheese
2	tablespoons plus 2 teaspoons virgin olive oil
1	teaspoon salt
6	cloves garlic, minced
2	tablespoons chopped fresh rosemary or dill
5 to 6	cups flour
	olive oil spray
1	clove garlic, minced for topping
	fresh herbs or kosher salt for garnish

Preheat oven to 375°.

In a large mixing bowl or food processor, dissolve yeast in 1/4 cup of the warm water. Let yeast sit 5 minutes or until it begins to bubble. Add sugar, cottage cheese, 2 tablespoons of the olive oil, salt, 6 cloves minced garlic, 2 tablespoons herbs, and remaining water. Blend. Add 3 cups flour and mix for 3 minutes. Add 2 more cups flour and blend again. Add enough of the remaining flour until dough is smooth and pulls away from the sides of the bowl. Remove dough and knead a few times. Cover dough and let rise in a bowl sprayed with olive oil spray until doubled in size. Punch dough down, cover, and let rise again.

Spray two 9 × 13 inch pans with olive oil spray. Divide dough in half and place into the pans. Stretch the dough to fit the pans, pressing the dough with your fingers to get the dough to the edges. Using your fingers, make dents in the top of the dough. Cover dough and let rise 30 to 40 minutes.

Brush the 2 teaspoons olive oil mixed with minced garlic on the top of the dough and sprinkle with some herbs if desired. If you are not worried about salt, you can sprinkle the bread with a little kosher salt. Bake for 20 to 30 minutes.

Each serving provides:

254	Calories	46 g	Carbohydrates
8 g	Protein	219 mg	Sodium
4 g	Fat	1 mg	Cholesterol
2 g	Dietary Fiber		

Pizza Dough

This dough will make a crisp, light crust. Use this dough in the following pizza recipes, or invent your own.

Makes 12 to 14 small pizzas
(1 pizza crust per serving)

1	package dry yeast
1/4	cup warm water (110°)
1/2	teaspoon salt
1	tablespoon baking powder
1	tablespoon honey
2	tablespoons nonfat yogurt
2-1/2 to 3 cups flour	
2/3	cup warm water (110°)
	vegetable oil spray

Put yeast and 1/4 cup warm water into a food processor with a metal blade. Pulse a few times and let sit until yeast begins to bubble, about 5 minutes. Add remaining ingredients, using only 2 cups of the flour to start with and adding the rest as needed to make a nice, soft, shiny dough. Put dough in a bowl that has been sprayed with vegetable oil spray. Cover and let rise 50 minutes. Punch dough down and let rest 10 minutes. Shape into little pizza rounds and top with toppings.

Each serving provides:

105	Calories	22 g	Carbohydrates
3 g	Protein	199 mg	Sodium
0 g	Fat	0 mg	Cholesterol
1 g	Dietary Fiber		

Vegetable Pizza

You can substitute any of your favorite vegetables to make this pizza your own. Be stingy with the optional cheese—1/2 teaspoon crumbled on top of each mini pizza adds plenty of flavor and not much fat.

Makes about 12 to 14 small pizzas
(1 pizza per serving)

	Pizza Dough (see page 174)
2	heads garlic, roasted (see Basics)
1	cup thinly sliced mushrooms
1	cup thinly sliced zucchini
1/2	cup diced green bell pepper
1/2	cup thinly cut cherry tomatoes
2	tablespoons Parmesan, feta, or blue cheese (optional)

Preheat oven to 425°.

Roll out 5-inch rounds of dough. Spread 1 to 2 soft, roasted garlic cloves on each round of dough. Spread mushrooms, zucchini, bell pepper, and tomatoes on the pizza. If you don't have an oven brick, lay pizzas on cookie sheets lined with baking parchment or sprayed with vegetable oil spray. Bake until crust is lightly browned, about 15 to 20 minutes. The tomatoes may be put on after the pizza is cooked if you prefer them uncooked.

Each serving provides:

128	Calories	27 g	Carbohydrates
4 g	Protein	226 mg	Sodium
1 g	Fat	0 mg	Cholesterol
1 g	Dietary Fiber		

Garlicky Lettuce and Tomato Pizza

I ate a lovely pizza similar to this in Italy—light, fresh, and delicious. You can get very creative with pizzas and still keep the fat down.

Makes about 12 to 14 small pizzas
(1 pizza per serving)

	Pizza Dough (see page 174)
2	heads garlic, roasted (see Basics)
3	cups romaine lettuce, slivered
3	tomatoes, seeded and diced
1/4	cup freshly slivered Parmesan cheese

Preheat oven to 450°.

Roll out 5-inch rounds of dough. Prick dough with a fork. If you don't have an oven brick, lay pizzas on cookie sheets lined with baking parchment or sprayed with vegetable oil spray. Bake until rounds are slightly brown, about 15 to 20 minutes. Squeeze out a couple cloves of roasted garlic per pizza and spread them on the dough. Cover each pizza with lettuce, a sprinkling of tomato, and a few shavings of Parmesan cheese.

Each serving provides:

140	Calories	28 g	Carbohydrates
5 g	Protein	263 mg	Sodium
1 g	Fat	2 mg	Cholesterol
1 g	Dietary Fiber		

Spicy Corn Bread

A scrumptious, moist corn bread with a robust flavor. I like to bake my corn bread in a heavy cast-iron skillet.

Makes 12 servings

1	cup all-purpose flour
1/2	cup cornmeal
1/2	cup cake flour
1	tablespoon sugar
1	teaspoon salt
1	tablespoon baking powder
1/4	teaspoon baking soda
1/2	teaspoon smoke flavoring
5	cloves garlic, minced
1	cup corn kernels, drained if canned
1/3	cup diced green chilies
1	cup lite evaporated milk
1/3	cup nonfat yogurt
1/4	cup egg substitute
2	egg whites
	vegetable oil spray

Preheat oven to 400°.

Sift first 7 ingredients into a bowl. Add remaining ingredients, except egg whites, and mix well. Beat egg whites until stiff and fold into batter. Pour into an ovenproof pan that has been sprayed with vegetable oil spray. Bake for 18 to 20 minutes.

Each serving provides:

121	Calories	23 g	Carbohydrates
5 g	Protein	376 mg	Sodium
1 g	Fat	4 mg	Cholesterol
1 g	Dietary Fiber		

Garlic and Dill Muffins

These light, savory muffins are delicious served with chicken, turkey, or main-dish salads.

Makes 12 servings

1	cup cake flour
1	cup all-purpose flour
1	tablespoon baking powder
1	teaspoon salt
1	teaspoon pepper
1	tablespoon minced fresh dill
4	cloves garlic, minced
1/2	cup fatfree sour cream
3	egg whites
1-1/2	cups nonfat milk
2	tablespoons grated Parmesan cheese

Preheat oven to 400°.

Mix the cake flour, all-purpose flour, baking powder, salt, and pepper together. Stir in the dill and garlic. Whisk the sour cream, egg whites, and nonfat milk together and stir into flour mixture until dry ingredients are just moist. Stir in Parmesan cheese. Fill 12 paper-lined muffin tins 3/4 full of batter. Bake for 12 to 15 minutes.

Each serving provides:

99	Calories	18 g	Carbohydrates
5 g	Protein	358 mg	Sodium
0 g	Fat	1 mg	Cholesterol
0 g	Dietary Fiber		

Garlic and Sour Cream Biscuits

These biscuits make delicious appetizers when filled with smoked turkey, cranberry sauce, and watercress. Baking parchment can be found in specialty food stores.

Makes 10 servings

2	cups flour
1	tablespoon baking powder
1	teaspoon salt
4	cloves garlic, minced
1	tablespoon dried sage, rosemary, *or* basil (optional)
1	cup plus 1 tablespoon nonfat milk
1/2	cup fatfree sour cream
1	tablespoon grated Parmesan cheese

Preheat oven to 400°.

Blend flour, baking powder, salt, garlic, and optional herbs. Stir in 1 cup milk and 1/2 cup sour cream until dry ingredients are just wet. Do not overmix. Dough will be sticky. Turn dough out onto a floured surface and sprinkle some flour on top of dough so it can be handled. Press the dough down with your hands to about 1-inch thick. Cut into 10 rounds with a cookie cutter and put on a parchment-lined cookie sheet. Brush each biscuit with some milk and sprinkle a little Parmesan cheese on each one. Bake for 12 to 15 minutes or until golden brown.

Each serving provides:

113	Calories	22 g	Carbohydrates
5 g	Protein	398 mg	Sodium
0 g	Fat	1 mg	Cholesterol
1 g	Dietary Fiber		

Basics

This chapter has instructions for basic techniques used throughout this book. The processes are called for so often that, rather than repeat myself, everything is in one spot for you.

How to Defat Broth: Refrigerate broth overnight and then discard fat that accumulates and thickens on top of broth.

Homemade Beef Broth:

1-1/2   pounds beef ribs
1   pound beef brisket
1-1/2   pounds beef shanks
2   chicken wings
1   onion, cut in half and skin left on
3   inside ribs of celery with leaves
8   cloves garlic
1   carrot cut in half
        a handful of fresh parsley
4   whole black peppercorns
        sprinkling of salt

Preheat oven to 350°.

Put all ingredients into a roasting pan. Bake for 2 hours. Fill roasting pan halfway with water and bring to a boil. Transfer all ingredients to a large stockpot and cover with water. Bring to a boil, turn down to a simmer, and simmer for 2 hours. Remove meat and strain broth. Refrigerate broth overnight and discard all fat. Broth can be used immediately or put into containers and frozen.

Homemade Chicken Broth:

1   3- to 4-pound chicken
4   chicken wings
2   carrots cut in half
3   celery ribs with leaves
1   onion, cut in half and skin left on
6   cloves garlic
6   whole black peppercorns
        a handful of fresh parsley
        few sprigs of fresh marjoram
3   bay leaves
        sprinkling of salt

Preheat oven to 350°.

Put all ingredients into a roasting pan and bake for 1-1/2 hours. Transfer all ingredients into a large stockpot and cover with water. Simmer for 2 hours. Strain stock and refrigerate overnight to remove fat. Shred and save chicken meat for other recipes.

How to Roast Garlic: Preheat oven to 300°.

Cut top off garlic bulb just far enough to expose garlic. Put into a small ovenproof container just big enough to hold the garlic. Spray the top of the garlic with olive oil spray and sprinkle with salt and pepper. Add 3 tablespoons of beef or chicken broth to the container. Cover with heavy foil and bake for 1-1/2 hours or until garlic is soft. Remove and squeeze out cloves.

Blanching Garlic: Separate cloves, leaving on skins. Toss into boiling water and let cook 5 minutes. Remove from water and peel. Now use garlic as you wish. The blanching makes the garlic a little milder tasting and is good for certain recipes that call for large amounts of raw garlic.

Baking Sliced or Slivered Garlic: In many of these recipes I have sliced the garlic very thin or slivered it for garnish. I like to bake the slivered garlic to give it a lighter taste. You must be very careful when you bake it and watch it closely. If it turns too brown it will be very bitter tasting. So watch carefully until it turns a *light* golden brown.

Preheat oven to 300°.

Put the sliced garlic on a small pan sprayed with vegetable oil spray. Spray the garlic with the vegetable oil spray. Bake, stirring often, until golden (about 3 to 4 minutes).

Roasting Peppers: Hold peppers with tongs over an open flame or put in the broiler and char on all sides. Immediately put peppers into a reclosable plastic bag and zip bag closed. Let peppers sit in bag 5 to 10 minutes and then peel.

Egg White Wash: Mix one egg white with 1 to 2 tablespoons water.

Cooking Beans to Use in Recipes: Sort dried beans and put into a bowl. Cover with water and let sit overnight. (If you do not have time for this, cover beans with boiling water and let sit 2 hours.) Drain beans and cover with fresh water. Salt water and add 1 onion cut in half for flavor. (The onion can be removed when beans are cooked.) Simmer until tender, about 2 to 3 hours depending on the kind of bean. Drain and use in recipes. (Do not drain if making baked beans.)

Homemade Noodles:

4	large eggs
2	tablespoons water
2	teaspoons olive oil (optional)
3	cups flour
1	teaspoon salt.

Put all ingredients into a food processor. Process until mixture starts to stick together. Remove and knead until smooth. Roll out and form. You can dry the noodles and save in reclosable plastic bags, or you can use immediately.

If you do not have a food processor you can make the pasta dough in your mixer or in a bowl, using a wooden spoon to mix the dough. Any of these ways is equally as good. Using the food processor is just neater and faster. Remember that homemade noodles cook much faster than packaged noodles.

Homemade Garlic Noodles: Use recipe above but add 8 to 12 minced garlic cloves when adding the olive oil.

Homemade Oil Sprays: There are many varieties of vegetable oil sprays on the market today. They all help to cut fat and keep things from sticking when you are baking. The sprays cut fat because you get a thin, even coating on the cooking surface and so can get the same results using much less oil. The commercial sprays are vegetable oil, butter-flavored vegetable oil, and olive oil. Since I love to use oils like sesame, walnut, and avocado, I put my own oil into plastic spray bottles and they work just as well.

Index

International Conversion Chart

These are not exact equivalents; they've been slightly rounded to make measuring easier.

Cup Measurements

American	Imperial	Metric	Australian
1/4 cup (2 oz)	2 fl oz	60 ml	2 tablespoons
1/3 cup (3 oz)	3 fl oz	84 ml	1/4 cup
1/2 cup (4 oz)	4 fl oz	125 ml	1/3 cup
2/3 cup (5 oz)	5 fl oz	170 ml	1/2 cup
3/4 cup (6 oz)	6 fl oz	185 ml	2/3 cup
1 cup (8 oz)	8 fl oz	250 ml	3/4 cup

Spoon Measurements

American	Metric
1/4 teaspoon	1 ml
1/2 teaspoon	2 ml
1 teaspoon	5 ml
1 tablespoon	15 ml

Oven Temperatures

Farenheit	Centigrade
250	120
300	150
325	160
350	180
375	190
400	200
450	230

More Cookbooks from Prima Publishing

Lean Bean Cuisine
by Jay Solomon

The humble legume inspired Solomon, a cookbook author and former restaurateur, to create these healthful, lean, and sophisticated dishes. Drawing on flavors from around the world, Solomon's meatless dishes include nouveau soups, salads, entrees, and side dishes. Each recipe includes a nutritional breakdown.

101 Great Sauces—No Butter, No Cream, No Kidding!
by John Ettinger

Salsas, chutneys, marinades, and savory sauces are all the rage! Sauces are a fast and easy way to add more punch and flavor to grilled meats, chicken, and fish and to dress up an otherwise ordinary meal. But most sauce cookbooks are filled with complicated, heavy concoctions made with lots of butter, cream, and flour that can really load down a meal with fat and calories. *101 Great Sauces—No Butter, No Cream, No Kidding!* features simple and healthful sauces you can use to deliver flavor without all the fat. Each recipe includes a complete nutritional breakdown.

The Best 125 Pasta Dishes
by Susann Geiskopf-Hadler and Mindy Toomay

A mouthwatering collection of meatless pasta dishes, this cookbook draws on the authors' seasoned imaginations to expand your sense of pasta's possibilities. With its emphasis on fresh ingredients and tantalizing flavors, this book proves we can eat less meat without sacrificing enjoyment. Treat yourself and your family to delicious pasta sauces, soups, salads, and baked dishes.

To Order Books

Please send me the following items:

Quantity	Title	Unit Price	Total
_____	_____	$ _____	$ _____
_____	_____	$ _____	$ _____
_____	_____	$ _____	$ _____
_____	_____	$ _____	$ _____
_____	_____	$ _____	$ _____

Shipping and Handling depend on Subtotal.

Subtotal	Shipping/Handling
$0.00–$14.99	$3.00
$15.00–$29.99	$4.00
$30.00–$49.99	$6.00
$50.00–$99.99	$10.00
$100.00–$199.99	$13.50
$200.00+	Call for Quote

Foreign and all Priority Request orders:
Call Order Entry department
for price quote at 916/632-4400

This chart represents the total retail price of books only
(before applicable discounts are taken).

Subtotal **$** _____

Deduct 10% when ordering 3-5 books **$** _____

7.25% Sales Tax (CA only) **$** _____

8.25% Sales Tax (TN only) **$** _____

5.0% Sales Tax (MD and IN only) **$** _____

Shipping and Handling* **$** _____

Total Order **$** _____

By Telephone: With MC or Visa, call 800-632-8676, 916-632-4400. Mon-Fri, 8:30-4:30.
WWW {http://www.primapublishing.com}

Orders Placed Via Internet E-mail {sales@primapub.com}

By Mail: Just fill out the information below and send with your remittance to:

Prima Publishing
P.O. Box 1260BK
Rocklin, CA 95677

My name is _____

I live at _____

City_____ State_____ Zip_____

MC/Visa#_____ Exp. _____

Check/Money Order enclosed for $ _____ Payable to Prima Publishing

Daytime Telephone_____

Signature_____